Entrepreneur

ULTIMATE
GUIDE TO

Influencer
MARKETING

Entrepreneur PRESS®

ERIC BUTOW and STEPHANIE GARCIA

Entrepreneur Press, Publisher
Cover Design: Andrew Welyczko
Interior Design by Laura Boyle
© 2024 by Entrepreneur Media, LLC
All rights reserved.

This publication is designed to provide accurate and authoritative information in regard to the subject matter covered. It is sold with the understanding that the publisher is not engaged in rendering legal, accounting, or other professional services. If legal advice or other expert assistance is required, the services of a competent professional person should be sought.

Entrepreneur Press® is a registered trademark of Entrepreneur Media, LLC

Library of Congress Cataloging-in-Publication Data
Names: Butow, Eric, author. | Garcia, Stephanie, author.
Title: Ultimate guide to influencer marketing / by Eric Butow and Stephanie Garcia.
Description: Irvine, CA : Entrepreneur Press, [2023] | Series: Entrepreneur ultimate guides | Includes index. | Summary: "This book is a comprehensive resource that equips small business owners with the knowledge they need to effectively connect with influencers and harness the power of influencer marketing" -- Provided by publisher.

Identifiers: LCCN 2023047993 (print) | LCCN 2023047994 (ebook) | ISBN 9781642011630 (paperback) | ISBN 9781613084748 (epub)
Subjects: LCSH: Internet marketing. | Social media--Influence. | Internet personalities.
Classification: LCC HF5415.1265 .B887 2023 (print) | LCC HF5415.1265 (ebook) | DDC 658.872--dc23/eng/20231012
LC record available at https://lccn.loc.gov/2023047993
LC ebook record available at https://lccn.loc.gov/2023047994

20 21 22 23 24   5 4 3 2 1

Contents

Foreword by Neal Schaffer

Congratulations on your purchasing of this book, *Ultimate Guide to Influencer Marketing*.

You are embarking on a journey into what I like to call one of the most powerful yet least understood marketing channels: influencer marketing.

There are no better guides to have at your side on this journey than Eric Butow and Stephanie Garcia.

Eric is the author of literally too many books to count with two hands, but most importantly, he is the author of *The Ultimate Guide to Social Media Marketing* as well as *Instagram for Business for Dummies*. Influencer marketing has become, as you will learn, synonymous to social media marketing for many businesses, and although TikTok has emerged as a prime competitor, Instagram is still the number one social network where influencer marketing budgets are being spent.

I have personally known Stephanie for almost a decade, running into her at marketing conferences and seeing her on live streams over the years, and more recently having the pleasure of seeing her on stage on multiple occasions at VidSummit, the largest conference for video content creators and influencers. Stephanie brings the important experience and perspective of an influencer to this book, giving much-needed balance and advice on how to approach, engage, and ultimately collaborate with influencers in real life.

I wrote a similar guidebook to influencer marketing called *The Age of Influence* back in the midst of the coronavirus pandemic in 2020, but the world has changed since then and tactics have evolved. It is great to see the authors of this book making invaluable contributions to our understanding of influencer marketing, and more importantly for you, easier to understand and practically actionable for every entrepreneur and small business owner that consumes this book to the end.

It's important to have trusted guides when talking about influencer marketing. A lot has been said about fake influencers and money wasted collaborating in order to chase vanity metrics, but just like any other marketing channel, without the proper knowledge and strategy, you can easily be spending a lot of money for unintended outcomes.

Many also see influencers as only being bona fide celebrities, meaning that only big brands can truly afford to work with them. This misunderstanding prevents many small businesses from leveraging influencer marketing, an opportunity cost that is huge.

If you think about it, the smaller the business, the more you have to gain from influencer marketing. The reason is that people buy from brands and businesses they know, like, and trust, but if you are not known how do you get the word out about your business and thus become liked and trusted?

Until now, many businesses have focused their digital marketing on Google and Facebook ads, but we know as time goes by that we trust ads less and less, and these ad expenses can add up very easily. On the other hand, we realize that people spend most of their time online on social media, so there has to be a better way to engage with people where they are and convert them into customers.

In the world of social media, it is the content creators and other influencers who truly have the ears and eyes of communities that every small business should be tapping into. People don't necessarily trust ads, but they trust the creators that they follow and the communities that they are a part of. Being recommended by a community leader is the shortcut to generating massive brand awareness that will lead to increased sales in whatever niche you are selling your product or service into.

Understanding the immense value that influencers can have in your business, however, is only the beginning. Just like Rome wasn't built in a day, it takes time to truly develop deep and long-lasting relationships of value with influencers. Too many businesses look for shortcuts and, unfortunately, treat influencers as if they were programmable ad units. This can actually cause more harm than good, so you always want to be entering relationships with mutual trust and value. This is the secret to having sustainable success with your influencer marketing.

Like anything else in business and in life, the true ROI of relationships are long-term. Just as you will learn that we are shifting from the mega celebrity influencer to someone on the opposite end of the spectrum who we would call a nano-influencer, the business world is also beginning to understand that influencer marketing ROI can be exponentially greater when we develop longer-term relationships with influencers, treating them as brand ambassadors and ideally converting them into becoming our brand advocates.

While this book will equip you with all you need to begin or positively revise your influencer marketing strategy, I hope you'll remember that there are tremendous benefits to working with influencers outside of the additional eyeballs and clicks that your brand or content will receive. These community leaders have their finger on the pulse of your industry and can provide invaluable feedback to you on your products and company that alone might be more valuable than any type of sponsored content they produce.

Above and beyond that, however, I believe the biggest benefit of collaborating with influencers might just be the content that they create and your reused user-generated content across your digital presence. I remember a marketing consultant client of mine with whom I helped run an influencer campaign targeting mommy bloggers. What struck me most from that collaboration was the quality of visual content that these bloggers, many of whom were also nano-influencers on Instagram, were creating. I found that the content was better than my client's internal team was creating, and, more importantly, just seemed more authentic and relatable.

At the end of the day, an influencer's content, which is dripping with authenticity and relatability, is the gift that keeps on giving when leveraged strategically as part of your digital marketing.

Just like talking to a friend who has already seen the movie that you want to watch, I will stop here so that I don't give away the entire plot line of this book. I hope you share in my genuine excitement for you and your business as you begin to increase your collaboration with influencers to bring your sales to new heights.

Neal Schaffer
nealschaffer.com

Introduction

If attention is the most valuable currency, then influencer marketing is the ultimate asset for building a powerful brand. In the HubSpot 2023 State of Marketing Report (hubspot.com/state-of-marketing), influencer marketing grew into a $16.4 billion industry with the second-highest return on investment (ROI) behind only short-form video marketing.

So, it's no surprise that you picked up this book to learn the fundamentals of how to find and incorporate influencers into your marketing to supercharge your sales. But an online search quickly exposes a task that appears overwhelming. The list of results includes influencers on TikTok, on Instagram, on YouTube, top influencers for Generation Z, and top influencers in various industries. Where do you begin and how do you tailor your approach to reach your target audience effectively?

Once you've created a valuable relationship with one or more influencers, we'll show you how to create compelling and successful campaigns. How do you know if they'll be successful? We've got you covered with methods for measuring and analyzing performance so you can tweak your message over time and keep the momentum going.

What's more, we'll give you plenty of best practices for working with influencers and tips throughout every chapter about finding success in the ever-evolving world of influencer marketing.

What You Can Expect from the *Ultimate Guide to Influencer Marketing*

As you browse this introduction to *The Ultimate Guide to Influencer Marketing* in your local bookstore, you may feel skeptical about influencer marketing. Perhaps you know it's important for your business but don't know how to convince your doubtful boss or business partner. Rest assured, this comprehensive guide will teach you everything you need to incorporate influencer marketing successfully. By the end, you'll have a firm grasp on proven strategies and know exactly what to do to see real results.

You'll discover:

- Life is largely about finding the right match, so knowing where to find influencers and how to select the right ones to market your brand globally is key.
- You'll understand why using micro-influencers is often better for your budget and for attracting more engaged customers to your product or service.
- You'll learn strategies for crafting clear agreements to ensure you and your influencers share expectations, as well as best practices for maintaining open communication throughout the campaign.
- Discover how influencer marketing campaigns can complement your broader social media strategy, integrating seamlessly with your other channels.
  This guide provides effective methods to track campaign performance beyond leads by measuring your social media impact and calculating your overall return on investment.

Use this book as a reference guide for working with influencers. It contains a comprehensive resources list and glossary. However, you'll first need to understand why influencer marketing is worth the investment of time, effort, and funds. Let's go to Chapter 1 and find out.

Section 1

GETTING READY TO INTRODUCE YOURSELF

All the Reasons to Invest in Influencer Marketing

Influencer marketing is huge. And it's growing bigger and evolving each year with new algorithms, content types, and engagement strategies. Brands need to stay ahead of the curve by partnering with influencers and content creators who can help them expand their reach and boost their bottom line. You can't have separate content, social media, and influencer marketing strategies anymore because each strategy feeds off the other to build trust, followers, and, ultimately, sales. In 2024 and beyond, you need to have an integrated online marketing strategy that combines all three components into a unified system.

Content, social media, and influencer marketing have become three intertwined strategies. It's no wonder we can no longer think of them as distinct paths. Each step builds on the success of the one before: content sells with trust; social media deepens that trust through transparency; influencers leverage that trust to influence B2B and B2C purchasing decisions. Together, they form a circuit of authority and appreciation—the shared currency that grows any brand.

According to Sprout Social, an influencer has specialized knowledge, authority, and/or insight into a topic or industry that gives them sway over their audience. (sproutsocial.com/glossary/influencer/) Influencer marketing is a key component in that system because influencers help people find, be inspired by, and learn about new products and services. They help you reach a larger and more relevant audience and stand out in a crowded marketplace. When you work with influencers who share the same values as your brand and your target customers, you can increase engagement, brand recognition, and (most importantly) sales.

Amplify Your Marketing

That's a very high-level description of what influencer marketing does, but to help home in on how it can help your business and justify the time, money, and effort needed to implement a strategy, we have seven reasons that combine to form the acronym AMPLIFY that explains how you can leverage the trust and relationships influencers have built to benefit your brand.

1. ALLOW YOUR BRAND TO TARGET CUSTOMERS

This is a big one. Through relevant influencers, your content is placed in front of social users that are already interested in your niche. You don't have to spend additional funds on testing and finding your audience, because the influencer has already fostered this audience on social media.

2. MULTIPLY NEW OPPORTUNITIES

When your small business begins working with influencers, try not to think of them only as channels through which you can broadcast your message. Instead, look at them as partners in creativity and marketing who can help you create unique content that will engage your target audience. Influencers are valuable assets, not just because they can help reach more people effectively and quickly, but also because they enable you to create content that adds value to your brand's story.

3. PROVIDE VALUE TO YOUR AUDIENCE

Influencer content can provide a ton of value to your audience—when it's done correctly. For example, Espin, which is an e-bike startup, partners with influencers to develop evergreen videos to teach viewers about their bikes. From reviews that share the products' benefits to videos that show how to assemble each bike, shoppers will find a ton of useful information from Espin's creators. Influencers deliver content that solves problems, educates, and inspires your intended audience.

> **TIP**
>
> You may consider partnering with influencers on a commission basis, because when more people see their branded content, that means increased earnings for them—and that may make influencers more interested in working with you.

4. LEVERAGE TRUST AND RELATIONSHIPS

By sharing an influencer's content, you'll soon gain their attention, and they'll begin sharing your company content with others and putting your message in front of an actively engaged audience in return..

Annabelle Nyst, Senior Content Manager for Brand Social, said, "Think of it this way: on the one hand, you have a brand telling you how cool it is and how its product is far superior to anything else on the market. On the other hand, you [audiences] have an individual who you're already familiar with and whose opinions you trust and respect, telling you they love this brand's product. Which are you more likely to trust?" (blog.hubspot.com/marketing/benefits-of-influencer-marketing)

5. INVOLVE INFLUENCERS IN YOUR CONTENT STRATEGY

Repurposing influencer content can help fill in the gaps of your own content schedule. This works well in situations where you've run out of content ideas or simply need some quality content to publish on your website and/or social media pages.

Engaging with influencers means you can easily add interesting, relevant content to your page without spending hours creating your own material. You can also utilize influencers as a source of ideas and inspiration. If you're stuck for content ideas, connect with an influencer and ask them to come up with a few topics they think your audience would be interested in. This is particularly effective if the influencer has experience in your industry or niche so you know their content will be of high quality and relevance to your brand.

6. FOLLOWER GROWTH

By leveraging influencers' existing audiences to expand your company's social media reach, you expose your company brand to a wider audience that's targeted for your brand. An influencer's endorsement establishes trust in your business with that targeted audience, which can drive traffic to your website or landing page allowing you to capture email addresses. When an influencer endorses joining your email list, followers perceive your brand as reliable and valuable, and are more likely to join your list so they can get more information. You can further leverage this new list for other marketing efforts and campaigns

Some key ways influencers can help drive sales include raising awareness among their own followers who may not yet be familiar with the brand, generating interest by showcasing the product's benefits through reviews and stories, building trust by conveying their own positive opinions, and promoting special offers to motivate purchases on the brand's e-commerce sites such as Amazon and/or through the shopping cart on their website. The influencer leads by example, demonstrating how they use the use the product in their daily lives, which inclines followers to purchase it themselves to achieve similar results.

> **TIP**
>
> Ross Brand, a well-known live video host and strategist at Livestream Universe (livestreamuniverse.com/), said business owners need to realize that influencers are very busy people. To get their attention, he said, "make it as easy as possible for them to contribute. Prepare graphics, email and social copy, and anything else they will need to share your work quickly and effortlessly with their audience."

7. YIELD MEASURABLE RESULTS

You need to set clear objectives and key performance indicators (KPIs) for influencer marketing campaigns, track your progress, and continually optimize your strategies to achieve higher return on investment, better known by its acronym ROI.

Setting clear objectives and key performance indicators (KPIs) for influencer marketing campaigns is essential for small businesses for several reasons:

1. **Focus and Direction:** Clear objectives provide focus and direction to your influencer marketing efforts. They help you define what you want to achieve and guide your decision-making process. Without clear objectives, you may end up running campaigns without a specific purpose or desired outcome, resulting in wasted resources and ineffective strategies.

2. **Measurement and Evaluation:** Objectives and KPIs allow you to measure and evaluate the success of your influencer marketing campaigns. By setting specific goals and metrics, you can track your progress and determine whether your efforts are yielding the desired results. This data-driven approach enables you to make informed decisions, optimize your strategies, and allocate resources effectively.

3. **Return on Investment (ROI) Analysis:** Clear objectives and KPIs help you measure the ROI of your influencer marketing campaigns. By tracking metrics such as the number of email sign-ups, conversions, or revenue generated, you can assess the effectiveness and profitability of your campaigns. This analysis enables you to identify the most successful strategies and allocate your budget wisely, maximizing the return on your investment.

4. **Alignment with Business Goals:** Setting objectives and KPIs for your influencer marketing campaigns ensures alignment with your overall business goals. Whether you aim to increase brand awareness, drive website traffic, boost sales, or grow your email list, clearly defined objectives help you tailor your influencer collaborations and content to achieve those goals. This alignment ensures that your influencer marketing efforts contribute directly to your business's growth and success.

5. **Accountability and Optimization:** Clear objectives and KPIs hold you accountable for your influencer marketing campaigns. By establishing specific targets and metrics, you can assess the performance of your campaigns and identify areas for improvement. If you fall short of your goals, you can analyze the data, understand the reasons behind the underperformance, and make necessary adjustments to optimize your future campaigns.

6. **Efficient Resource Allocation:** Small businesses often have limited resources, including time, budget, and manpower. By setting clear objectives and KPIs, you can

allocate your resources more efficiently. You can identify the most effective influencer partnerships, focus on channels that yield the best results, and allocate your budget based on the campaigns that align with your objectives. This ensures that you invest your resources where they are most likely to generate a positive impact.

In conclusion, setting clear objectives and KPIs for influencer marketing campaigns is crucial for small businesses. It provides focus, allows for measurement and evaluation, enables ROI analysis, aligns with business goals, ensures accountability, and facilitates efficient resource allocation. By setting specific goals and metrics, small businesses can optimize their influencer marketing strategies and maximize the success of their campaigns.

You'll learn how to create an effective KPI and ROI tracker for your influencer marketing in Chapter 11.

The Impact of Influencer Marketing

The impact of influencer marketing on consumer behavior can be seen in the results of recent studies. Here are some valuable statistics that speak volumes about the power of influencer marketing and how it transforms customer acquisition and advertising strategies.

1. Research has shown that online influencers are better able to change their followers' attitudes and behavior toward a brand because they are perceived as more accessible, trustworthy, and intimate than mainstream celebrities. (*Advances in Social Science*, "Education and Humanities Research", volume 655, 2022)
2. One big reason why influencer marketing has momentum is because of ad blocking. Not only do people prefer to hear from influencers, but those people also actively block online ads. (insiderintelligence.com/insights/ad-blocking/)
3. Consumers are more likely to trust peer recommendations, as they're generally considered more trustworthy than claims made in brand ads, and social media influencers can be very powerful in this respect. Influencers are able to establish trust with their community of followers because they are viewed as experts. According to Nielsen, in its global Trust in Advertising Study in 2021, which surveyed 40,000 across 56countries, 88 percent of consumers said that they trusted recommendations from people they know, above all other forms of marketing messaging. (nielsen.com/wp-content/uploads/sites/2/2021/11/2021-Nielsen-Trust-In-Advertising-Sell-Sheet.pdf)
4. If a product is accepted within someone's social circle, that immediately boosts its reputation and affiliated connection, which means the strongest voices within any group have huge sway over that initial relationship. (socialmediatoday.com/news/how-social-media-influencers-can-impact-your-customers-purchase-decisions/569813/)

5. Social media users tend to be more affluent and more likely to recommend products to family and friends. Blogs and Facebook are by far the most effective outlets for influencer marketing, dwarfing YouTube, Instagram, and Twitter. 37 percent percent said blogs were their most effective platform, while 25 percent said Facebook. (on.emarketer.com/rs/867-SLG-901/images/eMarketer%20Influencer%20Marketing%20Report%202022.pdf)

6. The Influencer Marketing Hub State of Influencer Marketing 2023 report showed that 83 percent of their survey respondents cited in the report believe influencer marketing is an effective form of marketing. (influencermarketinghub.com/influencer-marketing-benchmark-report/#toc-6)

7. Don't ignore the impact of influencers. In 2022, 72 percent of consumers said their trust in influencers has increased, 66 percent said their purchasing decisions were often driven by influencers, and 64 percent said that influencers help them discover new brands. (forbes.com/sites/walterloeb/2022/02/03/influencer-impact-on-consumers-increasing--facebook-has-less-power/?sh=35cd0914bad2)

We'll share more about which social media platforms are best for you to implement your influencer strategy in Chapter 2.

How Much Will You Spend?

On March 30, 2023, Stephanie interviewed Indra Gardiner Bowers, CEO of the marketing agency 62Above, on Stephanie's recent Lights, Camera, Live podcast episode. (youtube.com/watch?v=6GuguPYyDo4) In that episode, Indra shared her insights not only on navigating the ever-changing landscape of influencer marketing, but also how much you should spend on influencer marketing campaigns.

You may think that one of the benefits of working with nano and micro-influencers is their lower cost. However, Indra noted that some brands think they can trade their product for something, but it's not the case anymore.

A Starting Point

Indra said that even nano-influencers, which are influencers who work with a smaller but highly targeted audience, have begun to realize their value based on their engagement rates and adjust their pay structure accordingly. As of this writing, clients can expect to pay between $1,000 to $4,000 per engagement for nano- and potentially micro-influencers, even if they provide the influencers with free products. Indra noted that macro-influencers with large audiences are paid way more than that. She added that every influencer is different, so there is no set amount you can count on for different categories of influencers. We'll talk more about rates and influencer worth in Chapter 7.

SAVING BY DOING IT YOURSELF

If you decide that you want to save money by managing your influencer marketing in-house, Indra suggests a two-step plan to get the most bang for your buck..

First, set a small amount of your budget aside to boost your social media posts, because she said that's the only way to be seen and find new followers.

Then find an influencer who aligns with your brand and isn't too big—10,000 followers or less. Be prepared to negotiate compensation with both trades and cash. The minimum budget you need to set for an engagement is $1,000. As you talk with your prospective influencer, be very clear up front about deliverables, including how many posts, stories, or reels there will be, if and how the influencer will use your social media accounts, and desired hashtags to use for the campaign. Stephanie also talked with Alessandro Bogliari, the cofounder and CEO of The Influencer Marketing Factory, to get a good idea of what an influencer marketing agency does. (theinfluencermarketingfactory.com/) Alessandro listed several important considerations when you create your influencer marketing budget:

- The budget allocation for influencer marketing is highly variable, potentially ranging from 5 percent to 90 percent of your total marketing budget. You can't count on a one-size-fits-all amount.
- It's advisable to begin with a smaller budget, preferably in the five-figure range, and scale up based on success.
- Diversification is crucial. Choose a variety of influencers across different platforms and with different styles.
- You should customize your content to fit the specific platform and influencer you're working with.
- Tracking the results of each influencer campaign is essential. Use specific tracking links for each influencer to measure sales, clicks to your landing page, and other metrics.

> **TIP**
>
> Indra suggested an alternative to cash payment: offering travel experiences. For example, instead of paying cash, agencies can send influencers to a destination and cover their accommodations, food, and activities. This can often be more valuable to the influencers than cash.

Yes, we will cover these topics Alessandro listed later in this book.

Don't Forget Logistics

Working with influencers also means you have to deal with the costs and logistics of staging events, though the amount of work varies. If your company sells consumer-packaged goods, the process is more straightforward: you need to focus mainly on shipping and distributing your products to your influencers so they can review them. There should be requirements for influencers when they review products and services, and we'll talk about them in Section 2.

When it comes to staging events, you can have an in-house team do all the planning and coordination or outsource the work to agencies that handle the planning and coordination of these trips. (If you're a small to medium-sized business, outsourcing may be your best or only option.) Agencies experienced with influencer marketing work with their clients to consider factors such as accommodations, transportation, and experiences before even approaching influencers.

Alessandro Bogliari shared six key areas his agency, and any agency worth working with, must cover:

1. **Influencer Identification:** "We use sophisticated platforms to understand the demographics, historical data and so on."
2. **Agreements:** "We go through legal agreements, and it's important to have an agreement with each different influencer with a scope of work that goes into great detail."
3. **Logistics:** "We put together all the logistics if needed, such as for influencer travel, shipping of products, and any other items we need for the campaign."
4. **Creative:** "We do the creative part and all the storytelling behind the campaign."
5. **Execution:** "Once we have everything in place, we make sure that everything goes smoothly."
6. **Analysis:** "At the end of the campaign, we look at all the data, we tell you the dos and don'ts for the next campaigns, we analyze the ROI of the campaign, and we tell you what the next steps are."

Working with an agency for influencer marketing can offer several advantages and disadvantages. First, let's start with the advantages:

- **Expertise and Experience:** Influencer marketing agencies specialize in this field and have extensive knowledge and experience in identifying suitable influencers, negotiating partnerships, and running effective campaigns. They are well-versed in industry best practices and can provide valuable insights and guidance to get the most out of your influencer marketing efforts.
- **Network and Connections:** Influencer marketing agencies often have established relationships with a wide network of influencers across different niches. They can leverage these connections to identify relevant influencers who align with your brand, which saves you time and effort in finding and vetting influencers on your own.

- **Strategic Planning and Execution:** Agencies can assist you in developing a comprehensive influencer marketing strategy tailored to your goals and target audience. They can handle campaign planning, content creation, and campaign execution to ensure a streamlined and cohesive approach. Their expertise in campaign management can help optimize results and minimize potential pitfalls.

- **Streamlined Processes:** Partnering with an agency can streamline the influencer marketing process. They handle tasks such as contract negotiation, influencer briefings, content approvals, and performance tracking so you can focus on other aspects of your business. This can save you time and resources, especially if you lack the internal resources or expertise to manage influencer campaigns effectively.

- **Performance Tracking and Reporting:** Influencer marketing agencies typically provide detailed performance tracking and reporting. These reports can provide insights into campaign reach, engagement, conversions, and return on investment (ROI). What's more, performance reports allow you to assess the success of your campaigns and make data-driven decisions for future marketing strategies.

Now that you know the benefits of working with an agency, here are some drawbacks you should be aware of before you dive in:

- **Cost:** Hiring an agency for influencer marketing services involves spending more money. Agencies typically charge a fee or a percentage of the campaign budget for their services. If you have a small business with a limited budget, this expense may make working with an agency impossible (at least for a while).

- **Lack of Control:** When you work with an agency, you give up some control over influencer selection, content creation, and campaign execution processes. Though agencies aim to align their strategies with your goals and brand identity, you may have less direct involvement in the day-to-day decision-making.

- **Potential Misalignment:** There is a possibility of misalignment between your brand and the agency's vision or understanding of your target audience. It is crucial to establish clear communication channels, provide comprehensive briefs, and ensure that the agency understands your brand values and objectives. (We'll talk more about creating a campaign brief in Chapter 10.)

- **Communication and Coordination:** Effective communication and coordination are vital for successful influencer marketing campaigns. Working with an agency adds an additional layer to the communication process, and miscommunication or delays in communication can impact campaign timelines and outcomes. It's important to establish clear lines of communication and ensure that expectations are understood by both parties.

■ **Limited Brand Familiarity:** Agencies may work with multiple clients simultaneously, which can limit their in-depth knowledge and understanding of your brand. This may result in a less personalized approach to influencer collaborations or content creation. So, it's crucial to provide comprehensive brand guidelines and collaborate closely with the agency to ensure that your brand's unique voice and values are accurately represented.

Ultimately, the decision to work with an agency for influencer marketing depends on your specific business needs, available resources, and the level of in-house expertise. It's important to carefully evaluate the pros and cons, consider your budget, and assess the potential benefits an agency can bring to your influencer marketing efforts.

Indra compared setting up influencer events to arranging a mini-wedding. From transportation and accommodation to organizing activities, every little detail matters. She added that influencers expect organizers to think of everything, so you should also consider that as you decide whether or not to hire an outside agency.

What You Learned

Now that you've reached the end of Chapter 1, let's review what you've learned.

You know about the seven reasons for amplifying your business with influencer marketing, including allowing your brand to target customers and multiplying new opportunities for your business. Influencer marketing provides new value to your customers when you leverage the trust and relationships you build with influencers.

When you involve influencers in developing your content strategy, you amplify your marketing by allowing your brand to target customers, multiplying new opportunities to gain customers, providing value to your audience, leveraging trust and relationships influencers have with their audience, having the opportunity to involve influencers in your content strategy, growing your followers, and yielding results that you can measure to design future influencer marketing campaigns.

You need to be prepared to spend money to work with influencers, and Indra Gardiner Bowers of 62Above noted that influencers expect to be paid well with both cash and experiences. What's more, you need to be prepared to handle the logistics of creating events for your influencers no matter where they are. Influencers expect you to get events right from beginning to end, and if your company can't do that, consider partnering with a company like 62Above to help you.

You may be wondering if your company is a good fit for influencer marketing. Chapter 2 will tell you you what products and services work well with influencers—and which ones don't.

What Platforms Work Best with Influencers

Over time, brands have recorded a lot more feedback from influencer marketing campaigns in terms of sales, interest, visibility, and profits. This research has led to more rock-solid influencer marketing strategies in the field.

One of the key findings that you need to consider is the size of an influencer's audience, the influencer's niche or area of expertise, if the influencer's values and beliefs align with your company's mission, and the platforms you use for influencer marketing.

B2B vs. B2C Influencers

You may think there are few if any differences between business-to-business (B2B) and business-to-consumer (B2C), but when you look past all the media coverage of consumer brands using influencers, there are many differences that you need to know about if you're a B2B company looking for an influencer.

THOUGHT LEADERSHIP

B2B influencers focus on creating content that educates and informs their audience about a product, topic, or an industry. They're more focused on creating valuable and original content that focuses on the substance, and in many cases the text is in long-form presentations including blog posts, white papers, ebooks, and infographics.

For example, Stephanie produced "Showrunner: Secrets from the Set" video series that she did with the livestreaming platform Ecamm in 2022 and early 2023. She taught their existing customers about how to become remote live video producers. The series of livestreams was repurposed into blog posts, made available as an ebook, and given to attendees at Ecamm's "Leap Into Live" virtual summit in May 2023.

This in-depth approach provides insights and/or solutions to business problems so readers can consider those ideas and make better decisions. What's more, long-form content is more searchable by Google and other search engines, which makes a B2B creator's content travel more widely on the web.

In contrast, B2C creators focus on content that's designed to engage the audience's attention, and those creators work to be entertaining.

THE FOUR PARTS OF THE B2B INFLUENCER MODEL

Leading online digital strategist Michael Brito (britopian.com/) created a four-part B2B Creators Influence Model that has four segments: creators, collaborators, curators, and content promoters. .

Creators

Here are some examples of B2B creator campaigns for a company:

- They create exclusive content to post on their social media channels, website, and/or blog.
- They create campaign content for a company's social media channels.
- They co-create video content with other creators and/or brands.
- They create video interviews with company executives.

Paid B2B creators may also participate in company and industry events and produce content based around those, such as spotlighting the company and its employees at a big industry event.

Though it's cheap to research B2B creators online, keep two things in mind: they are expensive to work with, and they're also selective about who they work with. You should be just a particular with the influencers you select.

Collaborators

B2B collaborators are like creators in that they have original thoughts, ideas, and expertise to share, but they share those ideas only on social media channels. They usually collaborate with other B2B creators or directly with brands.

Brands partner with B2B collaborators in the same way as they do with creators. That is, there is no difference between B2B collaborators and creators in terms of how campaigns are constructed and executed. And collaborators are just as selective as curators.

Curators

B2B curators do just that—they curate or repurpose content from other creators. They also add their own unique perspective to the ideas and expertise they curate. Curators act as the nodes that connect different creator networks. They connect different ideas, articles, reports, and influential people in a topic or industry together.

Curators publish content, so it may be a good idea to engage one in a campaign to show people the breadcrumbs and connection points curators provide so that you can position your brand as a leader in your industry. It takes time to research curators in your industry, but the connections they can bring to you can be a gold mine for many aspects of your business.

Content Promoters

B2B content promoters are the closest thing to a B2C influencer as content promoters have been using social media for a long time and understand what types of content perform well on each platform and build the strongest community.

Content promoters curate and distribute content and news differently for each social media channel. Where curators provide more context to material they curate, content promoters write their content to reflect trending news and topics. Unlike curators, who go into more depth about a topic they curate, a content promoter usually provides only surface-level details.

Here's an example of how your brand can work with B2B creators and then use a content promoter to help you amplify and bring it all together:

1. Your brand collaborates with three to four B2B creators to produce an influencer campaign.
2. The creators write blog posts, ebooks, and whitepapers that they post on their own websites and/or blogs, and post links on their social media accounts to those materials.
3. The creators livestream, produce videos, and participate in audio chats on such services as Twitter Spaces. (As of this writing, the service is still called Twitter Spaces even though Twitter has changed its name to X.)
4. At the same time, you bring on your content creators and also collaborate with one or more B2B content promoters who package and promote the creators' content in your influencer marketing campaign and your social media channels.
5. A B2B content promoter's strength is in creating engagement and driving traffic to your brand so you can make more sales. As with B2C influencers, B2B content promoters require a healthy budget to identify one who will work with your business on a campaign.

What are the Best Platforms?

In Chapter 1, we introduced you to Indra Gardiner Bowers of the marketing agency 62Above, and she said there are three platforms to consider when you're creating your influencer marketing strategy: Instagram, Facebook, and TikTok. In addition to those three, we include YouTube since you'll find a lot of influencers on that platform who are working with brands. Except where noted, the statistics in this section are from the eMarketer Influencer Marketing Report from 2022, which is the most recent version available as of this writing. (on.emarketer.com/rs/867-SLG-901/images/eMarketer Influencer Marketing Report 2022.pdf)

INSTAGRAM

As of this writing, Instagram sits comfortably in first place on the list of the top influencer marketing platforms U.S. brands use. As many as 76.7 percent of marketers are expected to use it for influencer marketing campaigns in 2023, a 4.1 percentage point annual increase. This dominance is expected to continue as we move into 2024. By then, analysts expect 80.8 percent of U.S. marketers to be using the platform for influencer marketing activities.

Instagram has had a significant impact on influencer marketing, transforming it into a thriving industry. Here are some ways Instagram has affected influencer marketing:

1. **Visual Content and Engagement:** Instagram's focus on visual content, including photos and videos, has allowed influencers to showcase products, lifestyles, and experiences in a visually appealing way. This visual nature of Instagram has greatly enhanced engagement and made it an ideal platform for influencer marketing.

2. **Growing Influencer Community:** The platform's user-friendly interface, easy content creation tools, and discovery features have empowered users to grow their audience, establish credibility, and collaborate with brands.

3. **Authenticity and Relatability:** Instagram has allowed influencers to connect with their followers on a more personal level. The platform's emphasis on authentic and relatable content has allowed influencers to share their experiences and recommendations in a genuine way. This authenticity has fostered trust among their followers and made influencer marketing more effective in influencing consumer behavior.

4. **Visual Storytelling and Product Promotion:** Instagram's features, including Stories and Reels, have provided influencers with various formats to engage their audiences and promote products or services. Influencers can leverage these features to create immersive and compelling storytelling experiences. What's more, the ability to add swipe-up on links and product tags in posts enables direct and seamless product promotion.

5. **Micro-Influencers and Niche Markets:** Instagram has given rise to the concept of micro-influencers, who have smaller but highly engaged followings in specific

niches. Micro-influencers allow brands to target niche markets effectively and reach a more targeted and relevant audience. Micro-influencers often have higher engagement rates and offer cost-effective options for smaller brands that have limited budgets.

6. **Influencer-Brand Collaborations:** Instagram has made it easier for brands and influencers to connect and collaborate. Brands can identify influencers who align with their target audience and values, and influencers can showcase their work and attract brand partnerships through their Instagram profiles.

7. **Data and Performance Metrics:** Instagram provides analytics for business accounts that allows influencers and brands to track engagement, reach, impressions, and audience demographics. This data-driven approach helps influencers and brands measure the effectiveness of their influencer marketing campaigns and demonstrate the return on investment (ROI).

One example of influencer marketing on Instagram is from popular travel blogger Simon Cohn-Gruenwald (@uwo), who has 138,000 followers. In 2021, he participated in an influencer marketing campaign with mpb.com, which is the largest global platform for buying, selling, and trading used photo and video equipment (see Figure 2-1).

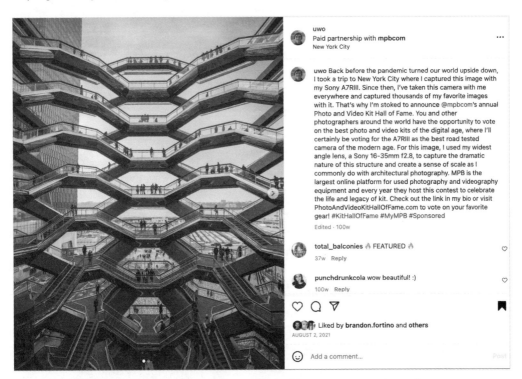

FIGURE 2-1. The Instagram post from Simon to promote mpb.com.

The team at mpb.com found Simon on Instagram directly. "The goal was to promote people to buy and sell used camera equipment on the site," Simon said. He added that he drove traffic to their site, but mpb.com didn't give him any statistics. We'll talk more about the importance of communicating with your influencer in Chapter 9.

FACEBOOK

Instagram is followed by social media giant Facebook, which is also owned by parent company Meta. According to HubSpot in 2022, 52 percent of marketers used Facebook for influencer marketing campaigns, and influencer videos accounted for 60 percent of video views on Facebook in the United States.

No, Facebook isn't as popular as Instagram, but you can amplify your reach by combining your influencer marketing videos with Facebook Ads to better target your video to your desired audience.

TIKTOK

TikTok is used by 50 percent of marketers as an influencer marketing platform. This is impressive considering the platform was launched in 2016, which is much later than the other top influencer marketing platforms on this list. Just three years ago, TikTok was used by 36 percent of marketers and was the fourth most-popular influencer marketing platform.

TikTok's popularity is forecast to continue rising and it is predicted that it will be used by 54 percent of marketers in 2024. According to a report by Oberlo, the TikTok boasts an average engagement rate of 13.7 percent which over 1 million influencers have—more than ten times higher than Instagram.

TikTok also has a TikTok for Business profile that provides videos about tips and inspiration for using TikTok and its advertising solutions, such as the video shown in Figure 2-2 from influencer Keenya Kelly.

FIGURE 2-2. Keenya Kelly talks about TikTok advertising solutions for the holidays.

YOUTUBE

YouTube is the largest video-sharing site on the Internet with over 2.7 billion logged-in users active on the site each month as of 2023. (globalmediainsight.com/blog/youtube-users-statistics/) As an influencer marketing platform, it's behind Instagram, Facebook, and TikTok. However, YouTube has a higher influencer engagement rate than Instagram with influencers who have over 5,000 followers. (oberlo.com/statistics/influencer-engagement-rate)

YouTube is also the second-largest search engine in the world, which isn't a surprise because Google, YouTube's parent company, says that at least 55 percent of consumers watch a video about a product or service before they buy it. (thinkwithgoogle.com/marketing-strategies/search/product-search-behavior-on-youtube/)

As you probably expect, YouTube's massive user base makes it a magnet for influencers to promote themselves in several ways:

1. **Accessibility and Reach:** Creators can show a wide variety of talents, expertise, and personalities to viewers. This has led to the emergence of a vast number of influencers across various niches and industries that attract dedicated subscribers.

2. **Authenticity:** YouTube fosters authentic connections between influencers and their audiences. Influencers share their personal experiences, opinions, and recommendations in their videos, which helps build trust and credibility among viewers.

3. **Diverse Content Formats:** Videos on YouTube give influencers the ability to offer a wide range of content formats including vlogs (video blogs), tutorials, product reviews, and even "day in the life" content. This variety allows influencers to showcase products and services in creative ways, and so it's easier for brands to collaborate with influencers and integrate their offerings naturally into the their video.

4. **Engagement:** Influencers can leverage their subscriber base and engage with their viewers through comments and likes, as well as viewers sharing their content with others. This engagement creates opportunities for brands to connect with their target audience.

5. **Monetization Incentives:** YouTube's monetization features including advertising revenue, brand partnerships, and sponsored content, have provided influencers with paths to generate income directly from their content. This incentivizes influencers to actively collaborate with brands.

6. **Analytics:** YouTube has built-in analytics tools so influencers and brands can analyze how their content performs. Metrics include number of views, watch time, likes, and audience demographics, which help influencers and brands gauge the effectiveness of their influencer marketing campaigns so they can adjust their strategies as needed.

Roberto Blake, who hosts a social media and marketing YouTube channel with over 500,000 subscribers (robertoblake.com), said that leveraging YouTube can directly convert videos to sales if you ignore some typical tenets of YouTube. Specifically, much of the content you see on YouTube is entertainment served as the product. Businesses that want to work with YouTube influencers to sell products and services need to prioritize customer-centric content.

Blake explained that this content needs to solve a problem in a definitive way and create a sense of satisfaction for your customers—one that will lead them to click on the link to your website in the video description to buy from you. What's more, he said, you need content that helps build community and credibility, and you need to find one or more influencers that can do that. For example, an influencer can show how to use your product and/or service in the real world, or your influencer collaboration can reflect the community you serve.

> **TIP**
>
> When you start talking with an influencer about YouTube videos, discuss who will host the videos. They can be on your company's YouTube channel, or you can have the video on the influencer's channel.

TIKTOK

TikTok requires a significant investment to create content on a regular basis, though TikTok viewers know that content can be rougher and more "behind-the-scenes" than on Instagram. TikTok has focused on forging strong partnerships with the marketing agencies that enabled brands across the country to propel their marketing. Here are some ways TikTok has influenced influencer marketing campaigns:

1. **Short-Form Video Content:** TikTok's primarily offers short-form video content that typically ranges from 15 to 60 seconds per video. This concise and visually engaging format challenges influencers to captivate their audience quickly and convey their messages effectively in a short span of time. The TikTok video format has led to the rise of TikTok-specific influencers who specialize in creating entertaining and engaging short videos.

2. **Viral Trends and Challenges:** TikTok is known for its viral trends and challenges, which quickly gain momentum and capture the attention of millions of users. Influencers often participate in these trends and challenges to show their creativity and gain exposure to a broader audience. Brands have capitalized on these trends by collaborating with influencers to create branded content that aligns with popular challenges and increases brand visibility and engagement.

3. **Discoverability and Algorithm:** TikTok's powerful algorithm allows content to be discovered and distributed based on individual user preferences and engagement

patterns. This has enabled lesser-known influencers and niche content creators to gain significant traction and reach on the platform.

4. **Authenticity and Relatability:** Many TikTok influencers show their unfiltered lives, which makes them more relatable to their followers. TikTok's casual and informal nature encourages influencers to be their authentic selves, which resonates with audiences. This authenticity has led to higher levels of trust and engagement and has made influencer marketing on TikTok effective in influencing consumer behavior.

5. **Diversified Content Categories:** TikTok encompasses a wide range of content categories that allows influencers to cater to a wide range of interests. Brands can collaborate with influencers in their common categories to reach a targeted audience.

6. **Interactive and Engaging Features:** TikTok offers interactive features including duets, stitches, and reaction videos that encourage user participation and engagement. Brands can leverage these features to encourage user-generated content, engage with their audience, and create a sense of community around their products or services.

7. **Cross-Platform Integration:** TikTok influencers often have a presence on other social media platforms, such as Instagram and YouTube. This cross-platform integration allows brands to leverage influencers' reach, engage their followers across multiple channels, and create a comprehensive influencer marketing strategy.

8. **Data and Analytics:** Like Instagram, TikTok provides analytics for creator accounts, allowing influencers and brands to track video views, engagement rates, follower demographics, and more. These metrics help influencers measure the success of their content and allow brands to evaluate the performance of their influencer marketing campaigns.

LINKEDIN

LinkedIn is gaining interest from influencers, especially those who promote business-to-business (B2B) products and services, in part because LinkedIn feels more legitimate compared to other platforms. One big reason is that LinkedIn turned twenty years old in May 2023, making it the oldest major social networking service still in use. (Facebook started in February 2004.)

Another big reason why LinkedIn is gaining traction with influencers is that it's built specifically with business networking in mind. It provides members with the best possible professional environment to connect with people and exchange their valuable knowledge. LinkedIn touts its audience reach by noting that 82 percent of B2B marketers achieve their greatest success using LinkedIn, and the LinkedIn audience has two times the buying power of the average web audience. (sproutsocial.com/insights/linkedin-statistics/)

LinkedIn influencers typically portray themselves as subject matter experts in a specific niche such as product development, leadership, content marketing, and advertising.

Influencers have spent years establishing their authority on LinkedIn by writing thousands of valuable posts and communicating with their followers, so chances are many of their followers trust them unconditionally.

Keep in mind, though, that developing a LinkedIn marketing strategy is no easy feat. With such effective reach to B2B buyers compared with other platforms, the environment is quite competitive and will require serious effort to secure good influencers for your marketing strategy. There are two strategies LinkedIn introduced recently that can help: collaborative articles and newsletters.

Collaborative Articles

In 2023, LinkedIn introduced collaborative articles that allow users and influencers to add their ideas, examples, and experiences to articles users can search for on LinkedIn. New collaborative articles also show up as notifications in your feed so users can read the entire article. (searchengineland.com/linkedin-collaborative-articles-launched-393866)

If you want to search for collaborative skill topic articles, follow the LinkedIn Skills Pages (linkedin.com/showcase/linkedin-skill-pages/) and then view all posts in the particular topics on the topic page. When you view an individual post, you can like and react to the article. Doing so automatically enters your request for an invitation to contribute to other articles. Over time, you can be recognized by LinkedIn as a top contributor by receiving a Community Top Voice badge for your profile.

"This type of content on LinkedIn is the newest and fastest way to get a notable badge on your profile," said Goldie Chan, a popular brand strategist, contributor to *Forbes* magazine, and a LinkedIn Learning Instructor. "While the community badges are constantly being reviewed on a month-to-month basis, LinkedIn also offers yearly badges in different categories," Goldie said. "Each of these badges can come from a variety of content types including video, newsletters, image or text posts and of course, the new collaborative articles."

What's more, she noted, "LinkedIn editors are constantly looking for fresh voices to feature and promote, so being active on the platform with high-quality, thoughtful posts that are specific to your niche, such as finance or marketing, will get you on LinkedIn's radar. I found my way onto the LinkedIn Top Voices list via videos, and now I explore many other formats."

LinkedIn Newsletters

LinkedIn users can also take advantage of long-form text to write articles of their own to keep readers up to date and to drive engagement. It's easy to write articles by clicking the "Write Article" icon at the top of the LinkedIn home page and then clicking "Create a Newsletter" to go through the construction steps. You can write your newsletter as yourself or as your company if you have a company page.

Lorraine Lee, who was the editorial lead for the LinkedIn newsletter product launch, stressed that your newsletter articles need to be genuine and open. For example, don't write about high-level company updates all the time. Instead, Lorraine says, "Any time you can tell a story and show what's behind the curtain, that's what will help you engage and grow your audience." (contentmarketinginstitute.com/articles/linkedin-newsletters-results-brands)

Is Your Business a Fit?

No matter what industry you're in, there are certain pitfalls that you need to avoid. Stephanie talked with Tyler Anderson, the founder and CEO of the Casual Fridays marketing agency, about his experiences and mistakes not to make before you determine if your business will fit with an influencer.

"There is value to working with influencers when done properly," Tyler said. "But most of my clients have felt burned at some point by self-proclaimed influencers only looking for free vacations. It takes diligence to ensure you choose quality influencers promoting your brand."

Tyler also identified two other significant mistakes brands make when it comes to influencer marketing. "Brands choose influencers based only on their follower count without vetting whether those followers are real or engaging," he said. "They also fail to have clear objectives and contracts in place. This leads to wasted budgets on influencers who don't deliver results."

Four Areas with More Influencers

If you take Tyler's experiences to heart and you're still interested in finding out if influencer marketing is a good fit for your business, research has made its way to media articles that shed light on different industries in the following four categories that work best with influencer marketing. (https://www.mavrck.co/find-influencers-in-your-industry/)

> **TIP**
>
> This doesn't mean that you won't find any influencers in areas other than these four. But if you're in the following areas, you may find a better fit with your company's message and vision.

HEALTH CARE

The health care industry is an essential business, and in most cases, professionals have face-to-face relationships with consumers and patients. People also look to the web concerning health issues, and influencers need to present a strong online image and give sound advice. What's more, there are FTC, FDA, and ethical standards that licensed health professionals need to follow.

All this means influencers need to be chosen carefully and have the right credentials to back up all medical claims made on social media. Trusted influencers are always sought by health care professionals to help spread the word about conditions and treatments.

FASHION AND BEAUTY

Influencer marketing has been a part of fashion and beauty marketing for generations in various media including print, radio, and television. Social media attracts those in Generation Z, which is the generation born between 1997 and 2012. A 2021 Statista report stated that 74 percent of Gen Z shoppers are driven by influencers when buying beauty products. (statista.com/statistics/1292842/impact-of-influencers-on-beauty-shoppers-in-the-united-states/)

TRAVEL AND LIFESTYLE

People who travel and create content that shows their lifestyle and what they use in their travels are natural influencers. Travelers show their experiences outside of brand messaging, and this gives them authenticity that companies can't match. The Millennial generation, those people born between 1981 and 1996, trust user-generated content 50 percent more than content generated by brands. (everyonesocial.com/blog/user-generated-content-statistics/)

TECHNOLOGY

Influencers are often at the forefront of the technology industry because they use a lot of the hardware and software they talk about in various media from podcasts to videos to text in articles and on forums like Reddit. Technology-focused influencers remain in high demand because of their knowledge as well as the education they provide about how to perform tasks and stay informed on the latest trends.

What You Learned

Let's review what you've learned in this chapter about the products and services that work best with influencers. We started by discussing the platforms that are the most popular for influencer marketing:

- Instagram
- Facebook
- TikTok
- YouTube
- LinkedIn

We also talked about why influencers use each platform, how each platform has affected influencer marketing, and the features that each platform uses to help both influencers and brands connect with their audiences.

Which types of businesses are best for influencers? It's likely you can find influencers no matter what industry you're in, but if you're in one of these four industries, you'll have a far better chance of finding plenty of quality influencers:

- Health care
- Fashion and beauty
- Travel and lifestyle
- Technology

No matter what industry you're in, you have to take care when you find influencers to make sure they provide accurate information as well as fit into your company's culture. Continue on to Chapter 3 to learn how to find the right influencers that fit with your business.

How to Fit Your Business with the Right Influencers

Finding influencers is a challenge no matter what type of business you have. Before you even think of finding an influencer, you need to stop, breathe, and ask yourself the questions listed below.

Define Your Goals

The question you need to ask is straightforward: What do you want to achieve by working with an influencer? Do you want to increase brand awareness, generate leads, or drive sales? Is the answer to that second question, "Yes"? Once you define your goals, you can start to look for influencers who have the reach and engagement to help you realize them.

Identify Your Target Audience

Who are you trying to reach with your influencer marketing campaign? For example, are they people who are interested in widgets that you offer, or a subset of the audience who want the widget that's your best seller and leads to upsells of your other products and/or services? When you know your target audience, then you can start to look for influencers who have a following that matches your target demographics.

Find Influencers Who Align with Your Brand

An influencer will represent your company, so it's logical that you need to work with influencers who share your brand values as well as whose audience is likely to be interested in your products or services. Do you know what your brand values are and how you want to communicate them to your audience?

Doing Your Research

Once you know what type of influencers you're looking for, now it's time to research potential fits with your brand, and this includes reading and viewing their written, audio, and/or video content to ensure they produce high-quality material with a consistent style that resonates with their audience.

There are many resources available to help assist you in your research. Combining methods and sources will increase your chances of finding the right influencer who can effectively promote your brand and engage your target audience. For example, if you want to find a YouTube influencer to promote your product and/or service on the largest online video site, you need to understand how to research YouTube influencers to find the right one for your brand.

The six red flags below come from Owen Hemsath, the co-owner of Acceleratus Media in the Salt Lake City area and a recognized leader in optimizing YouTube and video marketing for influencers and brands. Owen is on YouTube as Owen Video where he has over 400 tutorials that coach you about how to create videos, how to get the most from YouTube, and comments about the social media industry.

In a 2023 interview with Stephanie, Owen said there are six red flags you must watch out for when researching YouTube influencers and their videos:

1. Brands shouldn't evaluate videos in a campaign by views. Instead, they should analyze performance by the viewer's watch time. They should also note that watch time differs by video type, such as shorts, livestream, or a video longer than a minute or two.

2. Peak time is critical for when an influencer mentions the call to action in a video. Brands should see an influencer's analytics to see where views drop off and when the call to action (CTA) is mentioned.

3. Brands should limit how many CTAs are mentioned in a video. The CTA is the big ask and shouldn't be buried by other CTAs. So, ensure that the influencer understands this concept.

4. The B-roll in a video, which is secondary footage that provides context and visual interest in your story, should be exclusive to the brand. The influencer shouldn't use the B-roll in their other promo videos. Make sure your company owns that.

5. The number of video views can be inflated, which is why you want to measure the return on investment (ROI). Give the influencer a specific promo code for your videos so you can get an accurate ROI. (We'll talk more about calculating your ROI in Chapter 15.)

6. If a creator only highlights their subscriber count, total channel views, and mentions more than one CTA in a video, that's a huge red flag.

KNOW WHAT YOU'LL PAY

One thing you have to know before you start looking for influencers is how much you'll pay them. Influencers will want to be paid a healthy commission, which is something we'll talk about in more detail in Chapter 6.

For now, you need to calculate how much you can pay, and the SARAL influencer marketing platform has a spreadsheet on Google Sheets that's free to download so you can use it to figure out what your cost will be to sell your product, as well as the profit you'll make, in an influencer marketing campaign. *(docs.google.com/spreadsheets/d/1nsXlU5 4BszeqA2-SAI-D-PUilmLgoXixx5m9Gyc11bg/edit#gid=1490031815)*

This spreadsheet lets you plug in numbers in six different areas:

- Your product name.
- Your cost of goods sold.
- The total cost of producing the product, including shipping and packaging.
- Your product's manufacturer suggested retail price, better known by its acronym MSRP.
- The customer discount percentage you want to give the customers for using a promotional code during the influencer marketing campaign.
- The affiliate commission percentage.

After you add the numbers in these six spreadsheet cells, the spreadsheet calculates the totals in the remaining cells that show the influencer's affiliate commission for the product, your customer acquisition cost (CAC), your revenue, and the profit per sale from the influencer marketing campaign. The spreadsheet also shows you how much profit you'll see from 100, 500, and 1,000 sales of your product.

As you negotiate with an influencer, you can plug new numbers into the spreadsheet to see how high of an affiliate commission you're willing to tolerate and use that as a benchmark in your negotiations.

CHECK YOUR LIST TWICE

There are plenty of free blog articles online with helpful information For example, the website Notion isn't just about finding more information about their team collaboration app. They also have an influencer marketing vetting checklist for consumer brands that includes questions in three areas with titles that are themselves questions:

- Are their numbers where you want them to be?
- Does their content vibe with their brand?
- Do they have our audience?

You can read the entire Ultimate Influencer Vetting Checklist for Consumer Brands by following this link: https://getsaral.notion.site/The-ULTIMATE-Influencer-Vetting-Checklist-for-Consumer-Brands-1f9d3e00e43f4ac3bf05fc00bc845 5a.

KNOW YOUR HASHTAGS

Hashtags are vital to your influencer marketing campaign. You've undoubtedly seen them in social media posts with topic words preceded by a # symbol. They not only draw more eyeballs from social media users looking for those hashtag topics, but they also help you focus on what hashtags you want to promote (such as #organicskincare).

SARAL has a step-by-step Hashtag Research Strategy spreadsheet in Google Sheets to help you get the best creators for your brand, and you can download it for free. *(docs. google.com/spreadsheets/d/1TYanKI8GaG1O2byIzuEr16env5rOEFy4BHyGNs245BU/ edit#gid=114165508)* This spreadsheet has the steps in seven different spreadsheet tabs:

- The "Read This First" tab tells you how to use the guide and reminds you to focus on finding sources of influence, and when you broaden your search, you'll find better influencers.
- Your five hashtags that are core to your brand and tangential hashtags related to each core hashtag.
- The hashtags that reflect the experts in your industry.
- Recommended hashtags after you put your core hashtags on Instagram, and any other hashtags you find such as ones Instagram recommends.
- A couple of tool recommendations in SparkToro and Keywordtool.io to find influencers.
- A master list of influencers as the result of finding the right influencers that reflect the hashtags for your brand.
- A to-do list that includes finding at least fifty potential influencers in the first week after you have your master list.

The spreadsheet also has helpful links to other resources such as email templates for keeping yourself in front of your influencers.

ADD SARAL TO YOUR TOOLKIT

We've referenced SARAL's resources several times already because it's an invaluable influencer marketing tool. It's easy to use in Google Chrome by using SARAL's Chrome extension shown in Figure 3-1. You can use the extension as you browse YouTube, TikTok, and Instagram. When you visit an influencer's profile, the extension automatically analyzes and displays key influencer metrics like fair fees, predicted views, engagement rates, and diehard fans.

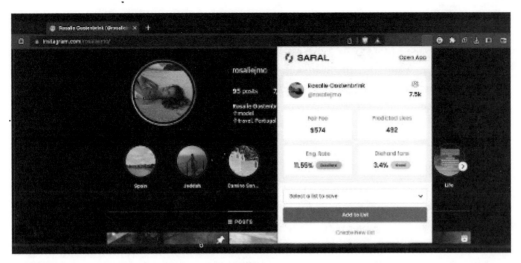

FIGURE 3-1. The SARAL extension shows influencer metrics in a pop-up window.

Another tool you can use in combination with SARAL is Creator Discovery from Social Native (see Figure 3-2). This tool allows you to search for influencers using a variety of different filters including the number of followers the influencer has, the influencer's location, and when the influencer last posted. You can also fetch the influencer's data so you can see how much engagement the influencer has.

FIGURE 3-2. The Social Native website allows you to book a free demo.

CONSIDER INFLUENCER MARKETING SOFTWARE

Research influencer marketing software that can help you find, vet, and manage influencers. Investing in a software program can save you time and money, and they can help you ensure that your influencer marketing campaigns are successful. Here are three leading programs to help you get started with your research:

Aspire

Aspire is a self-service search platform that allows you to match up with brands and 150,000 influencers on Instagram, TikTok, Pinterest, YouTube, and Facebook (see Figure 3-3). Aspire says they constantly add information to their search engine about influencers based on their social media posts, content quality, engagement, and more. (aspire.io/)

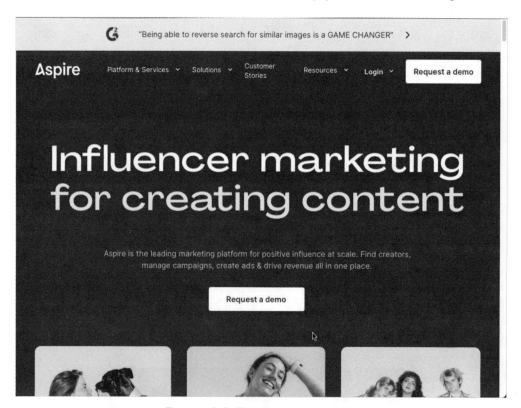

FIGURE 3-3. The Aspire website.

Upfluence

Upfluence, as shown in Figure 3-4, is a platform that focuses on bloggers and allows you to search for influencers based on their interests, demographics, and reach. You can connect with influencers as well as negotiate and finalize contracts directly in the platform.

And you can use Upfluence to track the performance of your influencer marketing campaigns. (get.upfluence.com/)

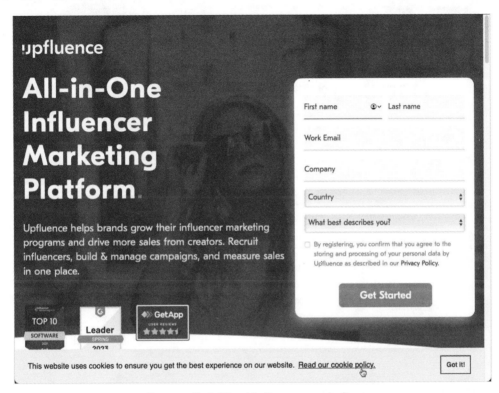

FIGURE 3-4. The Upfluence website.

#paid

#paid has developed an effective alternative method for quickly launching campaigns, matching businesses with the best creators, and whitelisting creator content (see Figure 3-5). To determine their ideal influencers, brands can create campaign briefs describing campaign goals and the scope of the desired content, as well as describe their ideal creator. What's more, brands can go further by whitelisting specific creators and content for use with paid Facebook and Instagram ads. (hashtagpaid.com/)

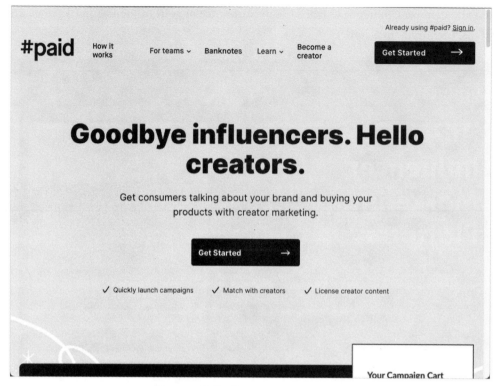

FIGURE 3-5. The #paid website.

SOCIAL MEDIA PLATFORMS

Social media platforms, including Instagram, TikTok, and YouTube can be valuable resources for finding influencers. Platforms have built-in search functions that allow you to discover influencers based on keywords, hashtags, and audience size. You can identify potential influencers by exploring relevant hashtags, engaging with their content, and following industry-specific accounts.

LOOK AT PAST COLLABORATIONS

When you research content from an influencer, review previous collaborations to see if they have worked with similar businesses or competitors in your industry. If they have, you need to analyze the success and

> **TIP**
>
> Influencer Marketing Hub has a good summary of twenty-four different software packages including the ones that we've mentioned here. You can find the summary on their website at:
>
> influencermarketinghub.com/influencer-marketing-software/

impact of those collaborations to find out if they were effective and if a similar collaboration could be effective for you.

INDUSTRY NETWORKING EVENTS

Industry-specific conferences, events, and other networking opportunities are great ways to find and connect with influencers in your niche. You can meet influencers face-to-face, discuss potential collaborations, and build relationships. Additionally, industry-specific online communities can be valuable resources for finding influencers and seeking recommendations.

REFERRALS AND RECOMMENDATIONS

Speaking of recommendations, don't just limit your search for recommendation to online forums.

Reach out to your professional network, colleagues, and industry contacts and ask them to recommend influencers they have worked with or know personally. That feedback can provide valuable insights and help you find influencers who have a track record of successful collaborations.

AGENCY PARTNERSHIPS

Influencer marketing agencies specialize in connecting businesses with the right influencers. These agencies can help you identify suitable influencers based on your specific goals and target audience. They often have established relationships with influencers and can handle campaign management on your behalf.

Beware of Influencers with Fake Followers

One unavoidable feature of the human condition is that when there is an opportunity for monetary success, some people will flout the system set up in place so everyone can benefit. In the case of influencer marketing, cheaters buy followers and likes to appear as legitimate influencers and deceive you into spending your money on them.

How do you spot a fake follower? There are five tell-tale signs to look for.

SPIKES IN FOLLOWER GROWTH

When an influencer's content goes viral, spikes in the number of their followers is a natural result. However, if a creator's follower growth looks more like a staircase or even a straight line instead of a curve, that's a sign you have to look more closely. When you see a big increase in an influencer's follower count and there isn't clear evidence why, that usually means the influencer is hiding the evidence that they've purchased their followers.

MANY LIKES, NO COMMENTS

When you research influencer social media profiles, always look to see how many likes and comments are associated with each post. At first glance, posts with a lot of likes look good, but look at the comments to see if there are any meaningful comments. If you see a lot of comments that are one-word responses like "love" and/or have a lot of emojis, the lack of meaningful engagement is a clear sign that the followers are not genuine.

LOW QUALITY AND LIMITED CONTENT

As you research influencers, you may find yourself asking why an influencer posts a terrible picture or has no point to the post except to post something. Combined with a high number of likes on the post, this is a clear sign that the poster isn't a legitimate influencer and you can move to the next candidate.

What's more, many influencers are active on more than one social media site. If the influencer is only on one social media site and there isn't a good reason for that, then that's a good reason to move along.

HOW DID THEY GET FAMOUS?

Every influencer becomes well-known to their audience for a reason, such as being a trusted resource for technology advice. So, when you come to an influencer's social media pages to check them out, one question you should ask early in your research is, "How did this person become famous?" If you can't figure out why that person is famous from their posts or if you can't answer that question from their posts, audio, and/or video, it's time to throw that influencer's name in the round file.

NO AVAILABLE ANALYTICS

If you're happy enough with what you've found about the influencer to start a conversation, don't forget to ask the influencer for the analytics of all their social media accounts. All major influencer platforms have audience statistics available for influencers that they can bring up and make available. If the influencer refuses to do this, then end the conversation. One popular tool is Social Blade (socialblade.com/), which allows you to search user and follower statistics for YouTube, Twitch, Instagram, and Twitter. This tool will also help you not only view follower spikes, but also confirm that what your influencer tells you about their user base is accurate.

A Cautionary Tale

If you don't take care in finding the right influencer for your campaign, the results can be costly to your brand not only in terms of money, but your brand's reputation. Eddie Garrison, the founder and CEO of Clover Media in Orlando, Florida, shared a story with us about when he managed a brand that didn't choose their influencer wisely:

A new axe throwing venue had recently opened and we were managing their social media presence from their opening through the first six months of operation. Around that time, their corporate offices reached out to us and said they had found a local (to the business) influencer they wanted to partner with to raise brand awareness through the influencer's audience and following.

Now here's where it got really interesting and honestly, this never should have happened. For some context, the axe throwing venue is a 21+ establishment that serves alcohol. Meaning you *must* be 21 years of age or older to even enter the building to participate.

The influencer the corporate office struck a deal with was a 19-year-old female makeup influencer whose largest following was on Instagram. Now to her credit, she did have over 100,000 followers on Instagram. However, the majority of her followers were females, under the age of 21, following her for makeup tips. Right there, this should have been a *huge* red flag that this was not the best partnership to run with for an axe throwing venue.

When the influencer arrived at the venue, the employees of the venue checked her and her friends as normal. However, none of them were over the age of 21. The employees ended up having to call the corporate offices to even get permission to let them into the building. This didn't start off the evening on the right foot.

After having all three of the influencer's party, including herself, sign underage waivers, they proceeded into the venue. Apparently, the influencer is not an overly athletic or physical activities type of person, and so she just sat in a chair most of the evening while her friends participated in the axe throwing. She never once threw any axes herself.

In the end, the influencer posted two images and went live on Instagram for around 10 minutes. This ended up garnering a few dozen likes and had a total of 11 people watch the live stream on her account.

When the live stream was shared to the axe throwing venue's Instagram account, their audience didn't even understand what was happening. Several direct messages came into the brand's Instagram account asking if the live stream was posted to their account by mistake.

Needless to say, this influencer partnership did not go very well at all, and it ended up costing the axe throwing venue more money than they wanted to spend on something that never materialized into any ROI for their brand.

What You Learned

Let's look back at this chapter so you can reinforce what you learned about how to fit your business with the right influencers.

Before you even start constructing an influencer marketing campaign, you need to ask yourself some questions. What do you want to achieve by working with an influencer? Who are you trying to reach through an influencer marketing campaign? Do you know what your brand values are so you can find an influencer who embodies those qualities?

After you answer those questions, you need to do your research. You can look at influencer marketing software to help make the process easier and more complete for you, and we gave you three examples to get you started. Look on influencers' social media pages to see how they work, and also look at their past collaborations.

Online forums, industry events, conferences, and other get-togethers are great places to ask for influencer referrals and recommendations. If all this sounds like too much, you can hire a professional agency to manage your influencer marketing campaigns.

An integral part of getting the right influencers is to find out how your business can get the most reach at a reasonable price point. In Chapter 4, we'll look at the different types of influencers and why micro-influencers have quickly become more popular with companies than large influencers with big audiences.

Section 2

MAKING VALUABLE
CONNECTIONS

Why Micro Is Coming In and Macro Is Going Out

Hiring an influencer will cost you money, and if money is an object, then you need to do your research to get the most bang for your buck. In this chapter, we'll tell you about the different types of influencers and how many followers each type has, the limits of traditional influencers, how your marketing campaign can make a big impact with smaller influencers, and how the authenticity of smaller influencers give your campaigns more credibility.

The Different Types of Influencers and Their Followers

Influencers are categorized into five groups by the size of their following:

- **Nano:** 1,000 to 10,000 followers
- **Micro:** 10,000 to 50,000 followers
- **Mid-tier:** 50,000 to 500,000 followers
- **Macro:** 500,000 to 1,000,000 followers
- **Mega:** 1,000,000+ followers

As you probably guessed, an influencer charges a different amount per post of content such as a video on YouTube or a reel on Instagram. And you're right, follower count dictates the amount influencers charge:

- **Nano-influencers:** $10 to $100 per post
- **Micro-influencers:** $100 to $500 per post
- **Mid-tier influencers:** $500 to $5,000 per post
- **Macro influencers:** $5,000 to $10,000 per post
- **Mega influencers:** $10,000+ per post

Breaking Down the Limits of Traditional Influencers

Even if you know that you can afford someone in one or more influencer categories, there are still limits in each category that you must be aware of.

1. Mega influencers, with their millions of followers, are typically reserved for large-scale campaigns because they're not always accessible for smaller budgets.
2. Macro and Mid-tier influencers, with smaller but still significant followings compared to mega influencers, can still be expensive. What's more, their large followings may mean that they have a lower engagement rate. Even though your product is getting in front of more eyeballs, not everyone will see it because as an influencer's follower count increases, the average engagement rate steadily declines.
3. With influencers in the micro and nano categories, they can be more cost-effective, but their smaller audience may mean that their reach is limited.

What About Smaller Influencers?

In recent years, there has been a shift toward micro and especially nano influencers because they're affordable and accessible.

Micro influencers have smaller followings, but they often have a more dedicated and engaged audience in a particular niche. For example, Figure 4-1 shows a good example from Toyota appealing more to an outdoor audience to sell its line of trucks.

FIGURE 4-1. James and Meg promoting Toyota on their Instagram feed.

Nano influencers can be more cost-effective to work with than larger influencers, especially if you're a small business or startup with a tighter budget. Yet brands may typically shy away from working with influencers that have under 10,000 followers because their perceived lack of reach may not get the best ROI. However, their targeted audience makes it

> **TIP**
>
> Because nano-influencers are usually just starting out, they may be willing to collaborate with your company in exchange for free products or services.

more likely that you'll home in on promoting your product or service to the demographic you really want to reach.

Take a look at this example from blogger Read With Sav. She recently partnered with the book-reading app Reckit (goreckit.com) on a post to promote some of her latest reads to her 3,500+ followers. If you look at her Instagram feed shown in Figure 4-2, you'll see a lot of comments and engagement. (instagram.com/read_with_sav_/)

FIGURE 4-2. The Read With Sav Instagram feed.

Small but High Engagement

Another key reason why micro and nano are coming in and macro is going out is nano influencers often have a high rate of engagement, which means that their followers are more likely to interact with their content. Nano-influencers have the highest average engagement rate with 4 percent across all feed posts, as well as sponsored ones. If we compare this to macro-influencers, they have an average engagement rate of 1.3 percent—three times lower than nano-influencers. (later.com/blog/influencer-engagement-rate/)

Authenticity

Arguably the biggest pro of working with nano-influencers is they're often perceived as more authentic and trustworthy than larger influencers.

Unlike larger influencers who may have a more polished or curated image, nano-influencers often have a genuine and relatable approach to content creation. They are seen as everyday people who have a passion for a specific niche, and their content reflects their personal experiences and perspectives.

For example, let's imagine a nano-influencer in the fitness niche who shares their weight loss journey and the impact of a particular brand's fitness program on their life. By openly discussing their struggles, progress, and results, the influencer establishes a genuine connection with their audience.

When they recommend the brand's program as a valuable tool, their followers are more likely to trust their endorsement because it comes from a relatable individual with similar tastes and preferences as they have—and who experienced visible results.

What You Learned

There are five categories of influencers: nano, micro, mid-tier, macro, and mega. Each category is defined by the number of followers the influencer has. The more followers an influencer has, the higher they charge.

However, a higher follower count doesn't mean you'll see better results with large influencers. Small influencers in the nano and micro categories often have more dedicated followers and higher engagement than large influencers. When more followers engage with content, the more likely it is that followers will be interested in working with your business.

Another factor in the growth of small influencers is that they're seen as more authentic with a passion for a specific topic. That enthusiasm radiates to their followers and gives the influencer''s recommendations more weight.

If you want to work with micro-influencers, Chapter 5 discusses how to connect with them and make them part of your marketing strategy.

Four Tips for Reaching Out to Micro-Influencers

Micro-influencers, which includes nano-influencers, aren't just for companies that are cost-conscious. Their engaged followers attract larger brands, including DoorDash, IKEA, and Starbucks (shown in Figure 5-1), who work with those small influencers consistently.

FIGURE 5-1. A nano-influencer talking about her experience at Starbucks.

Your business doesn't have the name recognition and respect of those big names, so how do you reach out to micro-influencers to start a relationship? Here are four tips we have for connecting with micro- and nano-influencers.

Do Your Research

There are no cutting corners when you search for micro- and nano-influencers who align with your niche, target audience, and your brand's values. Look for influencers who have an engaged following and create content that resonates with your niche and your brand. (You can bookmark this page and read Chapter 4 to learn where you find micro-influencers.)

For example, Verde Valle is a food company providing rice, beans, seeds, and lentil soups sourced from farms in Mexico and other sources in the world. Verde Valle's biggest competitor is Mahatma, which is a well-known brand in the U.S. In order for Verde Valle to make a statement in the U.S. market and establish their brand, Verde Valle brought in Claudia Sandoval, the winner of the Fox reality television series MasterChef, to promote their rice. Sandoval gave the brand credibility, which led to better brand awareness and more sales.

When an influencer and a brand don't mix, the fallout damages both. A recent example is fashion, beauty, and mom blogger Chriselle Lim when she sponsored Volvo's eco-friendly products. The message Volvo wanted to convey was to make people choose their products, but Lim's jet-setting lifestyle didn't fit that image since flying often isn't exactly eco-friendly.

Worse, Lim's followers immediately recognized that she was promoting eco-friendly products that were in fact not, especially Volvo's car cleaner. Lim looked disingenuous and the focus wasn't on Volvo's products. Both Lim and Volvo had to manage the fallout for their respective brands.

Engage First

Micro-influencers prioritize building authentic connections with their audience, so you need to approach them with a genuine intention to build a relationship. Before reaching out, engage with their content by liking, commenting, and/or sharing. Show your support for their work so you can become familiar to the influencer and their audience so you feel like your company will work well with the influencer. Then when you approach the influencer, it's more likely you'll get a positive response.

Personalize Your Outreach

Like all influencers, micro-influencers often receive numerous collaboration requests, so it's important to personalize your outreach so you can show your genuine interest in their work and the influencer will be interested in what you have to say.

Start by researching their page and their social media posts so you can understand their content, interests, and values. When you approach an influencer, mention specific aspects of their content that you appreciate and explain why you think a collaboration with them would be a good fit for them and your brand.

CRAFTING EFFECTIVE OUTREACH MESSAGES

Making a good first impression is crucial when reaching out to influencers. Your initial message sets the tone for the potential partnership. You want your outreach to grab the influencer's attention and excite them to collaborate.

But where do you start? With compelling subject lines, and you should aim for subject lines under sixty characters that feel personalized yet professional. Referencing their content and using their name can help.

Next, consider message length. Email messages from 100 to 150 words get the best response rates. Direct messages, better known by the acronym DMs, should be even shorter and more casual.

When it comes to email versus DMs, use emails for detailed pitches. DMs are great for short check-ins. Be aware that some influencers prefer one method over the other.

We have a number of email templates here that you can adapt for your needs when you want to reach out to one or more influencers. What's more, we have a link to these templates in the Resources appendix later in this book.

TWO GENERAL COLLABORATION EMAIL TEMPLATES

Here are two general email templates for collaborating with an influencer.

Example 1

> **Subject line:** [Name], we love what you shared on Instagram!
>
> Hi [influencer name],
> My name is [your name] and I work for [brand]. I loved your recent post about [related topic].
>
> At [brand], we make [describe product]. Since you often post about [topic], I thought you'd enjoy testing our product and sharing your thoughts with your followers.
>
> Let me know if you're interested in partnering!
> Thanks,
> {Your name}

Example 2

Subject Line: [Brand Name] + [Influencer Name] = Match Made in Heaven?

Hey [influencer name],
We love your Instagram feed! Your posts about [topic] are so [insert relevant compliment - creative, helpful, stylish, etc.].

I'm [your name], [fun position title] at [brand name]. We're all about [summary of brand] that helps [target audience].

Since you rock at creating [relevant content type] about [topic], we'd be so excited to collaborate! We'd love to send you our [product name] to try out and feature on your feed in your signature [adjective] style.

Let me know if you're interested in partnering up! I'm looking forward to hearing from you.

Cheers,
{Your name}

DIRECT MESSAGE EXAMPLES

When you send a direct message to an influencer, keep the tone casual as in these two examples.

Example 1

Hey [name]! We loved your post about [topic]. We think our [product] would be perfect for your followers. Want us to send you one to feature?
{Your name}

Example 2

> Hey [influencer name]! We loved your post about [relevant topic]. We think our [product] would be a great fit for your followers. Would you be open to us sending you one to try out and potentially feature? Let me know, would love to get your thoughts!

A BRAND AMBASSADOR EMAIL TEMPLATE

> **Subject Line:** Join our squad of [Brand Name] Insiders!
>
> Hey [influencer name],
> We absolutely love your Instagram feed and think your content would be a perfect fit for the [Brand Name] Insiders program!
>
> As one of our official ambassadors, you'd get to partner with us on special campaigns and content that align with our mission to [share your brand purpose].
>
> Some of the perks include [list two or three exciting benefits like free products, affiliate codes, etc.].
>
> We'd love to have someone as creative and passionate as you representing [Brand Name]. If you're interested in learning more about this opportunity, let's set up a call!
>
> Cheers,
> {Your name}

A BRAND AMBASSADOR DIRECT MESSAGE EXAMPLE

> Hey [influencer name]!
>
> We're gearing up to launch our new [product] and think you'd be an amazing brand ambassador for [brand]! Want me to send you more details?
>
> Cheers,
> {Your name}

BEST PRACTICES FOR INFLUENCER OUTREACH

When reaching out, use the contact method the influencer prefers. This is often listed in their Instagram bio or social media channels. If not specified, try email first.

Follow up if you don't hear back after one to two weeks. A simple "Checking in on my previous message about [topic]" message reminds them of your pitch.

Track your outreach efforts in a spreadsheet. List the influencer name, contact info, date of initial pitch, and any follow-up notes. This keeps things organized as your influencer list grows.

How many influencers you reach out to depends on your goals and available time. Outreach takes effort, so start small. Ten to twenty pitches per week is reasonable for most brands. Focus on quality over quantity.

The key is personalization. Mass blasting templated emails won't give you the results you want. Do research on each influencer before reaching out. Make it clear you value them and their audience. With persistence and the right approach, you can turn outreach into impactful partnerships.

AVOID THE TEDIUM

While manual outreach can work, it's incredibly time intensive. As your influencer marketing goals scale, this one-to-one process becomes unfeasible.

Platforms like Statusphere shown in Figure 5-2 can help streamline influencer discovery and activation at scale. Their tech matches brands with relevant creators through data-driven recommendations. This eliminates the need for tedious manual outreach.

FIGURE 5-2. The Statusphere website.

Offer Value and Benefits

Before you approach an influencer, write out the benefits and the value the influencer will gain from them. In your introduction, clearly outline the benefits they can expect, such as exposure to your target audience, product samples, exclusive discounts, and/or the opportunity to be part of a unique campaign. We go into more detail about how to do this in Chapter 6.

Clearly communicate your expectations, provide necessary details about the collaboration, and respond to any questions or concerns as soon as possible. At every opportunity, highlight how the collaboration will benefit both parties and build a long-term relationship.

When you show that you've put a lot of thought into your outreach and how you can work together, you'll have a much higher chance of success. Even if you don't succeed, you can get feedback from that influencer and the experience itself to have a successful connection with the next micro-influencer you approach.

What You Learned

Now it's time to summarize the four things you need to know about approaching micro- and nano-influencers.

You need to do thorough research to find not only micro-influencers, but ones that fit your niche, brand, and your company vision. Participate in the influencer's community so the influencer becomes familiar with you, and you can gauge if the influencer will be a good fit with your company. You need to offer benefits that show the value of your potential collaboration. And don't forget to act professionally at all times by communicating clearly and answering the influencer's questions and concerns in a timely manner.

When you're happy with an influencer, it's time to formalize your relationship. Chapter 6 goes into more detail about building a strategic partnership with influencers of any size.

How to Build a Strategic Partnership with Influencers

No matter the size of the influencer you want to approach, you need to put a great deal of thought into it. Many of the requirements discussed in Chapter 5 about micro-influencers also apply to all influencers:

- Define your goals and objectives for influencer partnerships before you even start researching influencer partnerships. Understanding your goals determines how you research and approach influencers.
- Engage with both the influencer and their followers by liking, commenting, and sharing posts. This helps the influencer become familiar with you and shows your interest in what they do.
- Personalize your outreach that shows that you've done your research, understand and appreciate their content, and value their expertise.

This is a good start, but your plan needs a complete structure before you present it to an influencer for consideration. Here are six components you need to include and share with the influencer to create a strategic partnership.

Craft a Compelling Value Proposition

Develop a value proposition that clearly tells the influencer about the benefits of collaborating with your brand. Highlight what the influencer stands to gain, such as:

- More exposure to the influencer's target audience
- Access to exclusive products or services from your company
- How much money the influencer will receive
- Any unique experiences your company can offer to the influencer

Most importantly, tailor your value proposition to address the influencer's specific interests and align it with their content and audience.

If you don't know where to start, Statusphere has created and shared a template on Google Slides so you can build a creative brief that you can send to influencers (see Figure 6-1). The template has spaces to add your brand information, images, and all the campaign details. *(docs.google.com/presentation/d/1K9f2XaHk3-4blMd8Tcj5BOEJzb82MQ2-l538ERWpeNM/edit?usp=sharing)*

FIGURE 6-1. The instruction slide for the influencer creative brief template from Statusphere.

Another option is to consider a platform such as Capssion (capssion.com/brands), so you can create a campaign and then invite influencers on the platform to participate if they agree to your campaign terms (see Figure 6-2).

FIGURE 6-2. The Capssion website for brands.

Establish Clear Terms and Sign Agreements

Creating an influencer partnership is a business transaction, so you need to have a written agreement that clearly defines the terms of the partnership, including deliverables, timelines, compensation, disclosure guidelines, and exclusivity arrangements.

There are a number of sections you should include in an influencer marketing agreement:

- A detailed scope of work
- Company aesthetic and branding guidelines
- What content will the influencer be publishing, where will the content be published, and how often
- Timeline and milestone details
- A list of things you don't want the influencer to talk about or include in the content
- Any other specifics relevant to the influencer campaign that the influencer needs to know about
- If content requires pre-approval by the brand before publishing
- Access to influencer data
- Compensation details

These are not the only terms you should consider including in your agreement. You can get more detailed information from a public article by Neal Schaffer, owner of the digital marketing consulting firm PDCA Social. (nealschaffer.com/influencer-contract/)

AI is also entering the picture. Stephanie has a blog post on her Lights, Camera, Live website that spotlights July (see Figure 6-3), a company that uses AI to help creators analyze their influencer agreements. (lightscameralive.com/blog/creators-demystify-brand-deals-using-ai)

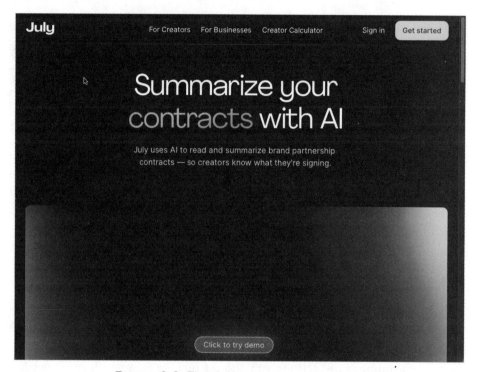

FIGURE 6-3. The July website home page.

Even after looking at online articles and drafting a written agreement, be sure you have your attorney and the influencer's attorney approve it before you and the influencer sign it.

Another AI-based contract scanner is Klaia's Contract Scanner on the Klaia website shown in Figure 6-4. (joinklaia.com/) The Contract Scanner generates contract summaries as well as customized negotiation email responses so creators can be better equipped to get the best terms possible.

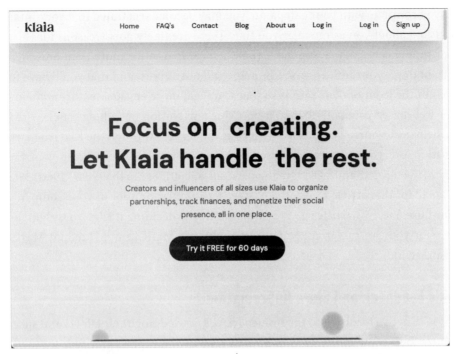

FIGURE 6-4. Klaia allows you to try their service free for sixty days.

Collaborate on Content Creation

Collaboration in content creation fosters a sense of investment in your relationship. As part of the partnership agreement, you should provide clear guidelines and expectations about how your company will involve the influencer. Allow room for their creativity and perspective so their authentic voice is part of your campaign.

Maintain Ongoing Communication

Open and frequent communication by both parties is essential if the partnership will be successful. For your part, you should check in with the influencer regularly, provide any updates, and offer support if needed. Team members in your business and the influencer are busy people, so setting up a regular meeting using an online chat program like Zoom or Google Meet should be a priority as the partnership launches.

> **TIP**
>
> Don't forget to include specific language about what has to happen for the agreement to end before its scheduled end date, such as behavior by either party that damages one or both parties. If the influencer refuses to sign with that language included, that's a clear sign to walk away.

As you continue with your campaign, you may become frustrated that your influencer isn't talking about you as much as you like. There are likely good reasons for this, such as your influencer is managing more than one campaign for more than one client. It's important to see your influencers as humans and not as bots, and that you'll have to keep yourself in the front of their minds so that you'll get more engagement from them.

The web-based productivity and notetaking app Notion has a blog article with a system to help keep yourself connected with your influencers through the Klaviyo marketing automation tool. (https://getsaral.notion.site/How-to-use-Klaviyo-to-keep-your-creator-community-engaged-and-get-regular-posts-out-a3c60178a71a4ba990c77196da38f38c) You can adapt this article to use the marketing automation tool in your company or, if you don't use one, this article can provide a gateway to deciding if Klaviyo is right for your business or you can research competitors including MailChimp, HubSpot Marketing, and Omnisend.

Provide Feedback and Show Appreciation

Offer constructive feedback to the influencer, acknowledging their efforts and successes. Recognize their contribution to your brand's growth and express gratitude for their partnership. Building a positive and mutually beneficial relationship will encourage future collaborations.

Track and Measure Results

Your partnership agreement could also include how you will monitor the performance of your influencer marketing campaigns. For example, you may specify that you'll use agreed-upon tracking software to track such metrics as reach, engagement, and sales generated by the partnership. Review these results on a set schedule with your influencer so you can work together to make future campaigns more profitable for both of you. We'll talk about measuring your campaign's return on investment (ROI) in Chapter 15.

What You Learned

Let's review what you learned in this chapter about building a strategic partnership with investors.

There are basic requirements for establishing a strategic partnership, including defining your goals and objectives, engaging with the influencer and their community before you reach out, and doing your research to personalize your outreach.

However, you need to do even more to convince an influencer to work with you. You need to create a compelling value proposition so the influencer clearly understands what they will get from the partnership.

A partnership is a business arrangement, so you need to sign an agreement that's vetted by attorneys for both parties. You must collaborate with your influencer on your campaign if your relationship will work even in the short term. Speaking of communication, you need to communicate with your influencer on a regular basis.

Don't forget to show your influencer some love for their efforts and also share your honest feedback about what's happening and how you think your campaigns can get better. As you track your results, that will help inform the feedback you give and get.

Part of learning about your goals and objectives for the partnership is to find out what type(s) of influencer collaborations work best for your company and the influencer. Chapter 7 lists a number of collaborations other companies use to create effective influencer marketing campaigns.

Types of Influencer Collaborations

There are plenty of ways you can collaborate with an influencer to reach your target audience.

You may have seen some of these yourself, and you can use one or more of these with a single influencer as well as use different collaborations with different influencers.

As you look through the following common collaboration types, remember that you need to select one or more types that align with your goals, target audience, and budget. You can tailor each type of collaboration to suit the needs of your business and the influencer's strengths.

Affiliate Marketing

Influencer collaborations using affiliate marketing involve influencers sharing unique referral links or discount codes for your product or service with their audience. When their audience makes a purchase using the link or code in a video or in text (such as the video description on YouTube), the influencer earns a commission. Affiliate marketing motivates influencers to drive sales and can be an effective way to track the impact of their influence on sales conversions.

There are also tools available to influencers to help them. Travis Brown, who you can find on Instagram @travisbrown, is a marketing influencer with 164,000 followers. He partnered with Stampede Social to generate over 1,000 hot leads in less than thirty days. Through captivating reels, he used Stampede Social's auto-DM feature to trigger a trackable automated affiliate link. Without any ad budget, he was able to convert 5 percent of leads into $30,000 in revenue from high-ticket coaching sessions.

Brand Ambassadors

Brand ambassador collaborations involve agreeing to a long-term partnership agreement with an influencer to become the face of the brand. Brand ambassadors promote your products or services consistently in their content, attend events, and advocate for your brand across various channels.

Event Sponsorship and Attendance

Businesses can collaborate with influencers by inviting them to industry events where the influencer plays a role such as hosting a panel, giving a keynote speech, or being a special guest in an interview on stage. This collaboration type helps increase your brand's visibility and credibility, as well as create networking opportunities between attendees, the influencer, and your company representatives.

TIP

In any brand ambassador agreement, be sure to set payment terms over the life of the agreement, such as the ambassador receiving more money over time and getting a bonus when you exceed the campaign goals. What's more, clearly detail what must happen for the agreement to end sooner than its expiration date.

Giveaways and Contests

Giveaways and contests are popular collaboration strategies. Influencers can host giveaways on their social media platforms where their followers can enter to win products or services from your company. This type of collaboration can generate excitement, engagement, and brand awareness.

Guest Content

You can work with influencers to create content for your brand's platforms, such as guest blog posts, videos, and content posts on your company's social media accounts. This type of collaboration allows your brand to benefit from the influencer's unique perspective and expertise while providing valuable content for their audience.

Product Development and Creation

If you sell products in your business, consider collaborating with influencers to create products or develop special edition items. Influencers can lend their expertise and unique insights about product features, design, and/or branding. This type of collaboration not only generates excitement about your brand, but also taps into the influencer's audience.

For example, Claudia Sandoval is a chef with over 115,000 followers on Instagram and was a contestant on the cooking reality show MasterChef. She worked on an influencer campaign with the Mexican food company Verde Valle (verdevallerecipes.com/en) to break into the United States market. Verde Valle's biggest competitor is Mahatma, and by working with a well-known figure like Sandoval, the company brought more visibility to their brand. (Unfortunately, Claudia couldn't share any specific numbers with us because she signed a non-disclosure agreement, or NDA, with Verde Valle.)

Social Advocacy

Your company may have one or more causes or social issues that it supports. In a social advocacy collaboration, you partner with influencers who align with your causes and/ or social issues. The influencer advocates for the cause and promotes the brand's efforts to get more people interested in the cause and make a positive difference in society. This type of collaboration can also help build brand loyalty and authenticity.

Sponsored Content

A sponsored content collaboration is one of the most common types of influencer collaborations. Companies pay influencers to create and share content featuring their products or services, such as a business that sells computer hardware for a tech channel on YouTube. In addition to video, the content can be sponsored posts, blog posts, dedicated product reviews, or a combination.

What You Learned

Now that we've reached the end of this chapter, let's review the types of influencer collaborations you can choose from, but choose wisely. They need to be the right fit for your influencer marketing campaigns.

Common influencer marketing types include affiliate marketing, brand ambassadorships, event sponsorships and influencer attendance at those events, giveaways and contests, guest content from the influencer, working together to create products, social advocacy, and paying influencers to sponsor your product or service.

> **TIP**
>
> In June 2023, the Federal Trade Commission updated their guide about using endorsements and testimonials in advertising. You can search for 16 CFR Part 255 or the matter number, P204500, on the FTC website at https://ftc.gov. The FTC website also has a business guidance page about this updated policy at:
>
> https://www.ftc.gov/business-guidance/resources/ftcs-endorsement-guides-what-people-are-asking

These may not be the only collaboration types you and your team can think of as you create your influencer marketing strategy. Once you know how you'll collaborate, read on to Chapter 8 to understand the roles of social media and content marketing. If you don't understand them, then you won't be able to build your influencer marketing strategy or learn how to craft your social media strategy, which is an integral component of your influencer marketing strategy.

Section 3

*PUTTING YOUR
INFLUENCER
MARKETING
TO WORK*

The Roles of Social Media and Content Marketing

Without having the rest of your social media plan in place to promote content about your brand, you won't be able to craft an effective influencer marketing strategy. Even if you already have content marketing in place in your business, reviewing this chapter is a good idea to make sure that you have all your bases covered and that you clearly understand the roles of social media and marketing your business content.

There are three things you should have in place before you start working on your first influencer marketing campaign: a presence on social media platforms that reaches your audience, a website, and a blog that you maintain regularly that people can access from your website.

Your website and blog provide in-depth information about your niche and industry so that your website isn't just found more easily by search engines, but also positions you as a leader in your industry that your current and potential customers should keep reading so they can make better decisions.

Social media is not there to market your website and your blog. In fact, marketing your website and blog shouldn't be a goal at all. Your marketing should be all about promoting your brand and using your platform to grow and educate your audience. Therefore, your website and especially your blog are part of your overall marketing strategy. Influencer marketing builds on the social media and

> **TIP**
>
> Having a lot of content to show potential influencers you want to collaborate with will go a long way toward having the influencer understand what your brand is all about and make it more likely that they'll be happy to work with you.

content work you're doing and have already done—or will do after you finish reading this chapter, right?

We may talk a lot about blog promotion, but by that we mean that you're using the blog, and the blog's content, as a tool to market your business.

This is an important point, because if you approach social media without a blog or content plan, you lose opportunities to leverage many of the benefits social media can offer. While determining your content plan is beyond the scope of this book, we'll assume you're prepared to create and use your website content accordingly.

So, the rest of this chapter will focus on how you can use social media and content together as a wonderful tool for building your business. Specifically, we will discuss a number of approaches where social media and content complement and enhance each other.

We'll start with how content can be used to create activity (shares) to your social profiles, which can deliver value and, of course, drive referral traffic. We'll use those shares to build authority and drive conversations. We'll then discuss how content and social media can be leveraged with influencers and other social media angles to achieve your business goals.

Social Sharing

Of course, the obvious way to market and promote your brand and content is through those initial social shares. But even then, just hitting all the buttons isn't the way to go.

Social media is not a broadcast channel for your business. It's a way for you to connect and engage with your audience, which means you need to share your new content in a way that's sociable and conversational.

On Facebook, X (formerly Twitter), Instagram, and LinkedIn, you have an opportunity to introduce your latest post and explain to your audience why they should be interested in reading it. It only takes a few minutes for you to write a sentence or three, and the result will be a dramatic increase in engagement and referral traffic.

Think about it. If you just spam your post to Facebook, you're relying on your post title, and perhaps an image (if you set it up right) to entice your readers. On the other hand, if you talk about why you've written the article, and perhaps ask a direct question, people will be more likely to take an interest. In this way, you'll be delivering value and interest right from the start, which will help to further your relationship.

Otherwise, you're just asking your connections to do you a favor, and you'll soon spend whatever capital you might have earned.

Of course, the obvious question here is, how do you know whether you're seeing a real ROI from your social media activity? Google Analytics, a free website reporting tool you can install from Google, will tell you where your referral traffic is coming from, and if you set up goals on Analytics, like online purchases, sign-ups, or contacts, you can see that, too.

Additionally, the major social platforms offer high-level insights on follower growth and engagement. We will spend a great deal of time discussing metrics and reporting tools in Chapter 13.

But if you want to get a clearer picture across multiple channels, you're going to need a social media management tool like Agorapulse. (agorapulse.com) You'll be able to track over time how your social campaigns are helping to build your brand awareness and authority, and ultimately contributing to sales.

Don't worry, we'll explain more about what Agorapulse is and what it does later on. For now, just know that there are tools available to you, both free and paid, native and third party, that will help you measure your success.

Authority Building

Now take a step back for a moment, and think about all the blog posts you share to social media. Are they on topic? If they are, then over time you should develop a reputation as an authority on that topic.

For example, XayLi Barclay is the CEO of the Start, Shoot, Grow marketing agency that has a large community of women entrepreneurs, and XayLi created a Thinkific course to help them build her clients' brand with video. XayLi was an enthusiast of Thinkific (thinkific.com/), which creates online courses and builds communities around those courses, and she caught the attention of the company when she posted an Instagram video promoting their platform as an affiliate. From there, XayLi became a Thinkific brand ambassador, and now she partners with them to host the Think In Color Summit, which celebrates female entrepreneurs and women of color.

Again, remember that social media's purpose isn't to promote business or content; it's to form relationships and develop them through conversations and discussions. And today, that exists in two basic forms: comment exchanges and live video discussions.

You can go into Facebook groups, LinkedIn groups, and other social media communities to find other people talking about your industry and relevant topics. You'll note that they're raising points, sharing content of their own, and most importantly, asking questions.

The most effective thing you can do with your blog content, and to promote your business overall, is to notice someone asking a question that you've already answered in a blog post, and direct them to it. Simply say, "Hey! That's a great question. I went in depth on that topic in this post: (insert link) and I think you'll find all your answers there. Check it out and let me know if you have more questions."

To the person asking the question, that's incredibly powerful. You just simultaneously demonstrated helpfulness and expertise, not to mention accessibility. That person is going to be very grateful and interested in what else you've written. They're much more likely than a random visitor from Twitter to share your post and subscribe to your email list. (And don't forget your comment on a public post will be seen by others as well!)

Similarly, livestreaming on Facebook, YouTube, LinkedIn, and Instagram offers the opportunity for multiple people to participate in live video discussions on whatever topics they wish. More on how this works in a moment.

Now, let's combine the initial social sharing approach we mentioned earlier and the authority building approach we just talked about.

Those initial shares to your social profiles are great, and in fact, you should be resharing your content to those social profiles on a regular basis (since you're always gaining new fans, and only a small fraction of your total fans would have seen the initial post). But even if you were able to get your blog content in front of all your followers, you'd still be talking about a relatively small number of people.

When you participate in other people's discussions or live video events, that's an opportunity to expand into larger groups of people who have potentially never heard of you. But the limitation there is that you have to wait for someone to post the right question or wait to be invited on someone's show. And those are opportunities that you simply cannot force or predict.

So that means it's up to us to spark some discussions of our own.

SOCIAL GROUPS

The first place to look for discussions to participate in is those same Facebook groups, LinkedIn groups, and other specialized communities. You can also include X (formerly Twitter) chats, Quora, and other online platforms where you're able to start a conversation around a topic.

Just as with the initial social sharing, you have to be clever and respectful when you go about this. These destinations are not simply places to broadcast your links. In fact, many social groups do not permit links at all. So, be mindful of whatever rules and requirements an individual group has in place.

(Note that most groups and communities have a pinned post or group description where the basic rules are laid out. Just remember that, for the most part, the group just wants to make sure it's not filled with spammed posts, and the posts are created for real discussion that benefits the group.)

The idea is simple. Start a new discussion based around the topic you've blogged about. You might ask a question that relates to the post, or, better yet, take a position that is somewhat polarizing and watch how people flock to one side or the other.

We've taken the time to identify and join all kinds of marketing and social media groups and communities on Facebook and LinkedIn so that every time we have a new piece of content, it's just a matter of finding the perfect community and the perfect angle through which to get a conversation going related to the blog post we want to share.

This brings up a really important point: don't wait until you have a relevant blog post or promotion to join communities. Start now.

Begin finding and joining communities that you think will be mutually beneficial, and begin participating in the conversations taking place. That way, when you're ready to share something of your own, you're not a complete stranger to the group.

For instance, if your business is focused on a specific geographic region, such as St. Louis, Missouri, take a few minutes to search Facebook and LinkedIn for groups of other professionals there. You might find general groups, like "St. Louis Entrepreneurs," where you will be able to connect with other professionals, as well as industry-specific groups like "STL Digital Marketers."

LIVE VIDEO

A somewhat similar slant involves the live video events that are going on constantly. At any time, you can see which Facebook, Instagram, LinkedIn, TikTok, or YouTube videos are live and start watching any that are of interest to you.

While the technical formats are different, the basic tenets are the same. One or more people will be participating in a live discussion and broadcasting their video and audio from their computers, while an unlimited number of viewers can be watching the live feed.

Audience members can chat with each other in the comments, mention that they liked something that was just said, or ask questions. Depending on the show format, participants can choose to answer questions live or perhaps come back and address comments after the show (if it's a more formal presentation).

Sometimes there will be questions that the show participants don't have the perfect answer for, and that's where you and your content come in.

As an audience member, you're free to share links to resources if appropriate. Of course, we don't want to just spam links to our own blog posts, so be judicious. And, just as with social groups, make sure that the first comment you make isn't a link to a blog post. You have to participate naturally, which means doing things like saying hi, asking some questions of your own, and so on.

Better yet, if you are a regular attendee to some shows (many people use Facebook Live to broadcast a regularly scheduled show that you can attend week after week), and you add to the show by participating and providing useful information, you may be invited to jump into an open slot during a show or perhaps be a featured guest in the future.

Spend some time familiarizing yourself with those platforms, and keep an eye out for others. Facebook Live and others are one-to-many broadcast platforms, so they work a little differently. We'll talk about this quite a bit in Chapter 13.

Broadcast Teaching

Yet another way that businesses can leverage social media, and live video in particular, is to teach a live audience about a topic.

On average, when giving a presentation, you'll deliver about 130 words per minute. That means an existing 1,250-word blog post will work out to a perfect ten-minute presentation.

Now, simply reading a blog post on a video platform like YouTube probably wouldn't be very interesting to your audience. But you can hit all the highlights of your post in about three minutes.

And three-minute videos are particularly popular.

The real beauty of videos, whether you're hosting a full-length show or making a quick Instagram broadcast, is that they can be repurposed. You can take a video from Instagram and upload it to YouTube and Facebook. You can pin it to Pinterest.

You can embed it on the original blog post or other blog posts, particularly if there's a short snippet that answers a specific question well. You can pull out the audio and use that for a podcast, further extending your reach into an untapped audience.

Sometimes you might even reverse the process: start with a video interview, and turn that into a blog post.

Dark Social Media

The one area you can't measure is dark social media. This refers to all the ways people can share your content with other people without your knowledge. Examples include emails, text messages, and direct social messages. In each of these cases, someone decided to share your content with one or more people, but they did so in a way that couldn't be accurately measured or recorded.

You can track dark social media by using links with UTM parameters to track when that link was shared in a direct message. UTM, or Urchin Tracking Module, contains five different URL (or web address) parameters that identify:

> **TIP**
>
> Agorapulse is a leading social media management platform that measures dark social media, and they have an entire article about dark social media and how to track it at:
>
> agorapulse.com/blog/what-is-dark-social/#how-do-you-measure-dark-social

- The site that sent the traffic.
- What type of link was used.
- A specific product promotion or marketing campaign, such as summer_sale.
- Search terms, such as walking+shoes.

- What was specifically clicked to bring the user to the website, such as a logo or text link.

You should make it as easy as possible for people to share your work this way if they want to. For instance, consider putting email buttons on all your blog posts. Or, better yet, just make sure that your social sharing buttons include an Other button that links to email, texting apps like WhatsApp, and whatever other choices someone might want to take advantage of.

Within your email newsletters, include social sharing buttons and an invitation to share the newsletter via email along with a note that says, "Did someone email you this newsletter? Make sure you don't miss another by subscribing yourself."

And, of course, make sure all your blog posts have a strong call to action to either read another post, head over to a landing page, or at least sign up for your email list so that you can further capture some of those dark social readers.

Paid Social Media

Finally, you should strongly consider incorporating paid social media in your marketing strategy. Every social platform now offers the ability to "promote" posts, allowing them to be seen by far more people than your existing follower base.

But be careful. It's easy to run up costs without seeing a real ROI. Make sure that you're using the best platform for your business, targeting the right audience, and sending that targeted traffic to the best possible content.

So let's bring this back to your latest piece of content. Think about who you're targeting with it. Is there a particular network where they're more likely to be active?

Frankly, one of the least expensive platforms to advertise on is Facebook. It also has the best targeting and sports the largest global user base. So that's probably a good place to start. But do give Twitter, LinkedIn, Pinterest, and Instagram due consideration. Chapter 9 will help you distinguish among advertising on the different networks, their content, and their audiences.

We find that the best content to promote on Facebook is content that's particularly strong for driving email sign-ups. Perhaps it has a content upgrade or related ebook that readers can download for free, creating targeted leads for your business.

A nice Facebook campaign, for just a few bucks a day, can send hundreds of readers and prospects to your blog post and business. So give that a try. Chapter 9 will show you how.

What You Learned

We know we've covered a lot of ground in this chapter—that was deliberate. We wanted to make sure you had a complete picture of how social media can be used to market your business and coordinate with your content. But we don't expect you to tackle all these techniques tomorrow.

Instead, start with social sharing, and take the time to get that right. Then move on to authority building, and so on. As you progress through the various strategies we talked about in this chapter, you'll find that it naturally follows your progression as a business marketer overall.

If you've just published your first blog post, you can't just skip down to influencer marketing. You have to have a consistent history of delivering quality content to establish the credibility you need to form relationships with influencers in your field.

Now that you've reached the end of this chapter, it's time to turn your attention to crafting your social media strategy if you don't have one in Chapter 9. Even if you have one, you may want to review it, but if you're happy with what you have, you can skip ahead to Chapter 10.

Craft Your Social Media Strategy

Your influencer marketing strategy can't succeed unless it ties together snugly with the rest of your social media strategy. If you don't have a social media strategy for promoting your influencer marketing campaign (not to mention your business in general) and to follow up on a successful influencer campaign on other platforms, then any momentum you've built with that influencer campaign will die on the vine and people will demand answers.

If you just need a refresher or you've decided to know how to build your social media strategy around your influencer marketing, this chapter is for you. We're going to determine your strengths and assets, create some goals, and then pull all that together into a viable social media marketing plan.

Determine Your Strengths

This section might more aptly be called "Determine Your SWOT." If you're not familiar with SWOT analysis, it stands for "strengths, weaknesses, opportunities, and threats," and it's a way for you and your business to self-assess.

While typically applied to your overall business, industry, and positioning, you should do a SWOT analysis specifically for social media and, if you wish, your overall online marketing plan (which includes your website, blog, and any other content marketing you do online).

You'll find strengths and weaknesses internal to your business, such as having someone available (or not) to manage social channels, writing experience, comfort level on camera, and so on. You'll also find opportunities and threats external to your business, which might include influencers in love with your brand or competitors that dominate the market.

Take the time to consider and write down all your brand's strengths, weaknesses, opportunities, and threats. If you have a team, give them a chance to weigh in. If you're a solopreneur, this would be a great time to form a mastermind group or board of advisers for yourself—some outside folks who will speak truth to you (more on that later).

To help you get started, we're going to give you some strengths and opportunities to consider (see Figure 9–1).

After you've identified your strengths, as well as the other elements of the SWOT analysis, you'll better understand what will be easy for you to tackle, or what may present a challenge for you; where you should allot your time and resources, and where you might need to get additional help.

But before we get into that, there are a few more determinations you should make.

STRENGTHS AND OPPORTUNITIES

STRENGTHS:	
Two plus hours per week available to spend on marketing	
Experience/skill writing or editing	
Experience/skill creating graphics	
Experience/skill creating video	
Existing brand style guide	
Existing brand values documented	
OPPORTUNITIES:	
Few competing brands active on social media	
Little/poor relevant video content	
Brand/industry that favors visuals (e.g., food)	
Wide range of available influencers	
Brand solves a commonly discussed pain point	
Few existing communities within industry/customers	

Figure 9-1. Strengths and Opportunities Worksheet

Determine Your Assets

While some SWOT exercises may include assets as strengths, we like to break them out separately when it comes to online marketing and consider things like profiles, apps, and equipment. Obviously having an existing Facebook Page fan base of 100,000 would be considered an asset. But already owning a DSLR or mirrorless camera you can use for photography or live streaming video is also an asset.

As you work through the rest of this chapter (and this book), you must take what we teach you and apply it to your own business, industry, and target audience. Sometimes we will present you with a choice, such as posting images or video, and you will have to decide which is better for your brand.

That is where it will help to have thought about your strengths and assets. If you know you're comfortable on camera and already own a good video camera, the decision to go with video becomes an easier one.

Take a moment to consider all the assets you currently have at your disposal. We've come up with a few ideas to get you started:

1. Existing social channels/audiences
2. Existing graphic design software (e.g., Adobe Photoshop)
3. Existing audio/video equipment (e.g., webcam, DSLR, mirrorless)
4. Existing library of media
5. Existing website/email subscribers
6. Available budget

While considering your assets, you might also think of additional strengths, weaknesses, opportunities, or threats. Update those lists as you go.

For instance, while you might consider a large Twitter following an asset, you may also realize that not having any presence on YouTube, Pinterest, or Instagram is a weakness, which should be noted as such.

Determine Your Goals

Start by identifying what your business goals are. Think about the nature of your business and what would make it a success, and follow the reverse of our digital marketing funnel. Are you looking for sales or referrals? Leads? Traffic? Brand mentions? Social followers?

Note and prioritize each goal.

Now think about some specific performance levels and how quickly you want to reach them. How many sales do you want to target? How many leads will you need to be able to convert that many sales? How much traffic will you need to generate that many leads?

You could use specific values here, like units or dollars, or you could employ percentage increases month over month or year over year. Or you could use all of the above. It depends on your business model and how you choose to measure your goals.

A good rule of thumb is to use the "one percent" rule: One percent of your traffic will convert to leads, and one percent of those leads will convert to sales. Over time, through testing and experimentation (and depending on your industry), you'll rise above that level. But for planning purposes, it's an acceptable place to start. It may seem daunting to think you need 1,000 visitors for just one sale, but we'd rather be pleasantly surprised because we overestimated than find ourselves disappointed and unprepared because we underestimated.

When it comes to social media, rather than place emphasis on specific follower counts or social signals, the preferred methodology is to watch for increasing trends. You want to gain followers each week and get more likes and shares, day after day. To that end, watch what you try on social media and pay attention to which techniques yield the most fruit.

By now you should have some notes that look something like this:

1. Sales—10 within first 30 days
2. Leads/email subscribers—1,000 within first 30 days
3. Traffic—10,000+ within first 30 days
4. Increasing brand mentions on social media
5. Increasing followers on social media

Of course, every business is different. Inexpensive products that target regular consumers are easier to sell than expensive B2B services. But you'll likely need less traffic and fewer leads to achieve profitability with a high-end offering. And remember that paid marketing and advertising can put you in front of targeted leads much faster than what you'd achieve organically.

The less money you have to invest in marketing, the lower your expectations may have to be.

Determine Your Plan

While we started by saying that having a strategy is critical, we should probably amend that to say that "having a plan is critical." And to create a successful plan, we should take a moment to review how all these pieces can work together to achieve results for your business. (We will include website content so you have the full picture of how social media works in tandem with the rest of your marketing.)

You may have heard of sales funnels in the past. Digital marketing works along the same lines. Here's a typical sales funnel:

Awareness

Opinion

Consideration

Preference

Purchase

Imagine the bottom of the funnel, the narrowest part or mouth: This is the point where your prospects decide to become customers. It might be an online purchase from your website, a clickthrough to an affiliate site, or a phone call to place an order. The details, of course, will vary depending on your business. This is what is known as the *conversion point* of the process.

As you move up the funnel, it widens to include pages within your site that educate the prospect on who you are, how you can solve their problems, and the specific products or services you offer. These are commonly referred to as landing pages, which are the *consideration point* of the process—when prospects are comparing you and your services with available alternatives.

Above that, the digital marketing funnel typically includes blog posts and other content within your site that visitors may read and later come back to. In this *discovery point*, prospects may be educating themselves about their problems as well as about you.

At the top of the digital marketing funnel, we have what we call "outposts." These are social media profiles and channels, guest blog posts, search engine listings, email, referrals, and so on. Through these mediums, prospects are at the *exposure point,* where they may be hearing about you and your services for the first time, or perhaps they're looking for information on a topic that you've addressed.

It's important to note that, unlike the traditional sales funnel, the digital marketing funnel continues beyond conversion. Since prospects who have become customers will continue to visit your website, read your blog posts, and subscribe to your emails, your marketing efforts contribute to ongoing customer relationships and retention, both of which are critical components of a sustainable business.

Exposure

Discovery

Consideration

Conversion

Customer Relationship

Retention

With those concepts in mind, and the collection of strengths, assets, and business goals you identified earlier, you can start to assemble your overall plan for a successful social media presence that delivers real ROI.

Earlier chapters set the stage for social media marketing by outlining today's networks and important concepts. The rest of our chapters will give you deep dives into specific tactics and approaches, including live video, chatbots, influencer marketing, and more. As you read through the remaining pages, continue to consider your marketing plan and how each new tactic might complement or enhance what you've already planned to do.

At a higher level, your marketing approach will be to create interesting and helpful content that educates readers on the subject, presents you as an authority, and puts them in a position to hire you or buy from you.

Of course, not every post and activity should be directly focused on generating sales. When it comes to social media, you definitely do not want to be too pushy with your messaging. Instead, recall that the top of the funnel is about exposure. Creating social media activity that generates dialogue is far more effective. Try to balance business content with consumer-focused content (articles, fun facts, behind the scenes, etc.) that will appeal to your target audience organically yet remains in line with your business model and industry.

That starts with creating content on property you own yourself: your website.

CONTENT SCHEDULE

First, decide how often you're going to add new content to your website. Whether it's in the form of pages or blog posts is up to you. But you need a publishing schedule, and initially it needs to be inviolable. If you allow yourself to stray from this schedule early on, it will be too hard to get back on track, and before you know it, you're way behind in your marketing.

Now, for a startup business and website, it's important to get rolling as quickly as you can, and that means a high rate of publication at first. Generally, we recommend at least three to five pages or blog posts per week for the first six months. After that, if things are going well, you can ratchet down to two to three per week, and then eventually down to one per week/month.

A few years ago, marketing platform HubSpot analyzed some business blogs and their relative search engine traffic and lead generation. On average, most business blogs began to see an exponential increase in search engine referral traffic after they'd published more than fifty pieces of content. Lead generation rose accordingly.

That means that typically, if you post just once per week, it will be a year before you begin to see real gains in referral traffic.

Note that if writing isn't your jam, you can absolutely create video or even audio content instead. However, you will still need to embed that media onto your site and surround it with text to give Google and your readers context. You might also consider starting with video and repurposing it into written content, which we'll cover extensively in Chapter 13.

CONTENT TOPICS

Next, think about what you're going to write or talk about. Again, this is going to be a combination of landing pages and blog posts (or videos, podcasts, etc.).

Your landing pages should focus on areas in which you are establishing yourself as an expert. For each main landing page, consider two to three topics on which you could write and add as subpages. And then, for each of those subpages, think about two to three blog posts you can write relating to those topics.

When you're through, you will have all your site's most important content mapped out. You don't have to write it all overnight, and you can certainly mix other blog posts into your publishing schedule as topics come to mind. But now you have a plan.

One of the great uses of keyword research tools is to brainstorm content topics. You can actually see the phrases (keywords) that people are searching on and use those to develop ideas for new pages or posts.

Try to tell stories as you write. Whether on your landing pages or in blog posts, stories bring your audience into the room with you, while you weave in details of your expertise.

SOCIAL MEDIA PRIORITIZATION

Next, think about the social networks you're going to be active on. There's no "right" answer here. Rather, there are a number of things to consider, such as:

- Which social networks are you already active on?
- Which social networks have an audience that seems best suited to your business?
- Which social networks favor the type of content you prefer or are able to create?
- Do you have a personal preference?

While considering those points, let's put the major social networks into tiers. While we think you should create a professional profile on every social network, you only need to maintain constant activity on one or two platforms. Like this:

- Tier One: Facebook, X (formerly known as Twitter)
- Tier Two: Instagram, Pinterest, TikTok
- Tier Three: LinkedIn, Google My Business, YouTube, SlideShare, etc.
- For Facebook, X, Pinterest, LinkedIn, and YouTube, you will need a cover photo: a custom graphic branded to reflect your business (and tie into your overall marketing image). For all social profiles, use a professional logo or professional-looking head shot for the profile image.

SOCIAL MEDIA ACTIVITY

Instructions on how to use each social network is outside our scope, as it would require a book in itself to outline techniques and best practices for even just the top five or six networks.

Here are the basics you need to keep in mind and integrate into your marketing plan.

1. Remember that social media is not an advertising medium. It's an opportunity for you to connect with prospects, readers, and potential partners. It's a place where you can share content and information, offer value and assistance, and create a reputation. Don't blow it. If you always think about how or whether a particular post will be interesting and helpful to your audience, you'll make good progress.

2. Every time you publish a new piece of content to your website, share it to social media. Once you've selected your top-priority network, research best practices for sharing to that network so that your shares look and perform optimally.

   Every social network has its own unique set of best practices, so be mindful of them. For instance, you might share new blog posts to Facebook or Instagram only once, but consider tweeting about them three to four times the first day, once or twice the second day, and then have them in a rotation to be routinely tweeted along with your other content. LinkedIn and Pinterest audiences may tolerate a second share later in the day, but no more.

   Any frequency you choose to adopt must be tempered by the size of your audience, the platform, and your posting history. If, for instance, yours is a new Twitter profile, talking about the same blog post, four times in a day would be too much. This is very much a case of using your best judgment!

3. When you're not sharing new blog content, share content and articles from other sources that will also be helpful and interesting to your audience. This is called *curated content*. The easiest way to do this is to identify several sources of information that regularly publish new posts and aren't direct competitors. You can then subscribe to their RSS feeds using Feedly. The RSS feed just shares new content, and a reader like Feedly allows you to see it (and even share it).

4. Prepare a series of business-related messages that you can use to remind your audience who you are and what you do. These will only be shared sparingly—perhaps once a week or month. But make sure you're including them. It might be a sales message, an invitation to subscribe to your newsletter, or just a link to follow you on your primary network.

You can now set a social media activity schedule that looks something like this:

- *Facebook*: New blog post share, 1 curated content share

- *X*: New blog post share, 4 curated content shares, 2 influencers retweets, 2 archived posts
- *LinkedIn*: New blog post share, 1 curated content share

Modify as needed to reflect your own network priorities and desired levels of activity.

Use a social media management tool like Agorapulse to schedule much of this activity in advance, leaving you free to focus on your day-to-day business needs. However, you will want to spend a little time each day on your most important social network connecting with others, commenting on posts, and simply engaging with people.

Also be sure to keep an eye out for comments and mentions from your followers and always respond and thank people in a timely fashion. How fast is necessary depends on your business and audience. A small retail shop can likely check in once or twice a day, while a business that consumers are relying on may need to make sure every hour is covered.

Airlines, for instance, must keep on top of their social channels for customer service reasons. Customers are turning to social media to be heard, and it's critical that you respond within a reasonable amount of time.

SEARCH ENGINE OPTIMIZATION

While SEO as a topic is outside the scope of this book, great SEO can actually help your social media presence. More organic traffic to your site and content will raise brand awareness, create more opportunities to grow your social following and community, and generate more organic shares of your content to new audiences.

So let's quickly go over some basics.

When it comes to SEO, as we mentioned before, one of the best things you can do is research your topics ahead of time using a keyword research tool, and then create content for those topics. We recommend a tool called SEMrush.

Beyond that, here are some general tips to keep in mind as you go:

- Register your site with a free Google Search Console account to monitor your site, see how many pages have been indexed, and submit a sitemap.
- Use your targeted keywords as often as possible while still sounding natural. Do not "stuff" them by using them excessively.
- Use lots of images, and use keywords in image filenames and alt tags. Not only does this help with search, content with more images is more likely to be read entirely and therefore shared more often.
- Don't worry about the keywords meta tag, but do fill in all other meta tags appropriately.
- Use SEMrush to routinely audit your site and note errors and issues that you may need to address.

SOCIAL MEDIA AND/OR SEARCH ENGINE PAID ADVERTISING

We're going to devote an entire chapter to paid advertising (Chapter 11), so we don't need to go into detail here on techniques. But for planning purposes, it's important to create a budget for paid advertising and understand how it can be used to support your plan and business goals.

All the major social networks offer paid advertising options to reach new audiences and promote your brand. You can also take advantage of search intent and put your problem-solving content and landing pages in front of search audiences when they're using Google or Bing to find answers.

Must you advertise to succeed on social media? Not necessarily. A lot will depend on your industry and what the competition is like, as well as your business goals and timeframe for achieving them. Generally you'll find that paid advertising is most successful when it's used to amplify great organic marketing activities.

In other words, study the rest of this book closely to learn exactly what kinds of social media activities will work best for you and your audience, do those, and then consider putting some money behind promoting and helping to spread that great activity.

Remember that your marketing plan is a dynamic and living document, designed to change and adapt and grow right alongside your business. If you decide to focus on, say, Facebook initially, that doesn't mean you can't shift to Instagram after six months. Figure 9–2 shows you a simple template for a basic marketing plan. Feel free to tweak it to fit your needs.

MARKETING PLAN WORKSHEET

My Business Goals
1.
2.
3.
4.
5.

My Business Assets	
Total Budget:	
Total Staff:	
Website:	

My Business Assets

Social Profiles:	
Materials:	

Content

Publishing Schedule:	
Landing Page:	
Subpages:	
Blog Post Topics:	

Social Networks

Tier 1:	
Tier 2:	
Tier 3:	
Sources:	
Influencers:	

Activity

Network:		Frequency:	
Network:		Frequency:	
Network:		Frequency:	
Network:		Frequency:	
Network:		Frequency:	

Targeted Keywords

1.

2.

3.

Google Ads Budget:			
Facebook Budget:			
Other Ad Budget:			

Tool:		Cost:	
Tool:		Cost:	
Tool:		Cost:	
Tool:		Cost:	

Figure 9-2. Marketing Plan Worksheet

This is where the measurement and learning comes in. If you treat every marketing strategy and technique as an experiment and open yourself to listening to the data, you will be able to make sound business decisions and smart changes in direction.

What You Learned

Before you create a social media strategy, you need to analyze your strengths, weaknesses, opportunities, and threats (SWOT). After your analysis, you can develop your goals for your social media campaign, and then develop your social media plans. Your strategy should not only include what to post and how often, but also consider related technologies including search engine optimization (SEO) and paid advertising. We also included useful worksheets for you to fill out for your own business.

Once you have your social media strategy in place to support your influencer marketing strategy, continue to Chapter 10 to learn how to build your influencer strategy campaign.

Build Your Campaign

Once you've signed an agreement with your influencer and you know what types of collaborations you'll use, it's time to construct your first influencer marketing campaign. This chapter tells you the steps you need to build your campaign and it's the one you may want to bookmark so you (or someone on your team) can refer to it as you start each new campaign.

Set Campaign Objectives

Job one is to clearly define your campaign objectives and what you want to achieve through the influencer campaign. Do you want to increase brand awareness? Do you want to drive sales of your product and/or service? Do you want to reach a specific target audience? Chances are that you'll answer yes to at least one of these three questions, and maybe think of a few based on the type of influencer collaboration(s) you're using. Once you set your objectives, they guide the rest of the campaign planning process.

Stay Informed and Adapt

You, and/or someone on your team, need to continuously stay informed about influencer marketing trends and industry changes. Your influencer is probably already doing this and can contribute a lot of helpful information about what will work with their ever-evolving audience desires. Adapt your campaign accordingly to ensure that it's relevant and effective.

Understand Your Audience

Your influencer's audience may have been exposed to numerous influencer campaigns in the past, so you need to look at your interactions with the influencer's audience prior to your collaboration with the influencer. Talk with your influencer about how to address issues they may have about what their audience wants so that they don't post a rolling eyes emoji in the comments to tell you they're bored and skeptical about what you have to offer. Doing your homework will inform your content choices and give you a better chance of creating an authentic and engaging message.

Create a Campaign Brief

An influencer marketing campaign brief is an essential document that outlines the goals, guidelines, and

expectations for a brand's partnership with an influencer. A clear, thoughtful brief sets both parties up for success by ensuring everyone is on the same page about what needs to be accomplished.

A brief acts as a roadmap that guides the influencer in creating content that aligns with the brand's messaging and reaches the intended target audience. It provides key details on campaign objectives, content specifics, timelines, and compensation so there is no confusion about deliverables.

There are eight key sections that every influencer marketing campaign brief should contain. We'll look at providing an overview of the campaign, defining goals, specifying the target audience, highlighting brand messaging, setting content guidelines, mapping out a timeline, explaining compensation, and outlining how campaign success will be measured. Having these elements thoroughly mapped out in the brief ensures the influencer has all the necessary information to produce great content for your brand.

CAMPAIGN OVERVIEW

The campaign overview section provides high-level details on the influencer marketing initiative. This includes the campaign name, the dates it will run, which social media platforms will be utilized, and the types of content that will be produced. For example, the overview could state:

- **Campaign Name:** Summer Fun Giveaway
- **Dates:** July 1 - August 31
- **Platforms:** Instagram, TikTok
- **Content Needed:** Two sponsored posts per platform featuring our new line of sunglasses. One post should focus on an unboxing video, the other on a summer outfit pic featuring the sunglasses.

Giving concise overview information orients the influencer to the basics of the partnership right away. They'll know the campaign name, when it will take place, where their content will live, and the general content expectations. Having these key details spelled out upfront ensures the influencer has the right context to dive into the rest of the campaign details.

GOALS

The goals section clearly defines what the brand aims to achieve through the influencer marketing partnership. Having specific, measurable goals gives the influencer direction on how to shape their content to deliver the results the brand desires. Potential goals to outline could include:

- Increase brand awareness among the target 18- to 24-year-old female demographic
- Generate 500,000 video views across TikTok and Instagram
- Drive a 10 percent increase in sales of our new sunglass line via affiliated links
- Produce user-generated content showing our sunglasses being worn that can be reshared
- Grow Instagram following by 5 percent and TikTok following by 10 percent
- Achieve 3 percent engagement rate across sponsored posts
- Activate 15,000 sweepstakes entries for a giveaway

Defining the campaign goals gives the influencer clear direction on the business objectives their content needs to help accomplish. With specific goals outlined, they can craft posts designed to drive the desired awareness, engagement, and conversion results.

TARGET AUDIENCE

The target audience section outlines details on the specific demographic and buyer persona the brand aims to reach with the campaign. Defining this helps guide the influencer in shaping content that will resonate best with the intended consumers.

For our sunglasses campaign, the target audience is:

- Women aged 18-24
- Located in the U.S.
- Interested in fashion and accessorizing
- Active on social media and influencers
- Enjoy summer activities like the beach, festivals, and concerts
- Value uniqueness and self-expression
- Budget-conscious but willing to spend more on trendy items
- Likely students or entry-level professionals

Providing these psychographic and demographic details gives the influencer insight into the mindset, values, and interests of the target consumer. This allows them to take an audience-centric approach to crafting compelling content using relevant messaging, styles, and specifying the target audience so the influencer can steer the campaign results with content tailored for maximum impact.

MESSAGING

The messaging section identifies two to three core brand themes or values that should be incorporated into the influencer's content. This ensures the posts align with the overall brand identity and desired positioning.

For our sunglasses campaign, key messages to convey include:

- Our sunglasses are an affordable way to make a fashion statement. Their unique, eye-catching designs let you showcase your style without spending a lot.
- Our sunglasses are tailored specifically for the young, socially conscious consumer. We use sustainable materials and practices to cater to this demographic's values.
- Our sunglasses are made for summer adventures. Whether heading to the beach, a music festival, or just out with friends, our eyewear is durable and stylish for all your warm-weather fun.

Calling out a few concise brand messages gives the influencer direction on weaving in relevant themes that resonate with our target audience. This allows them to create authentic content that communicates our positioning.

CONTENT GUIDELINES

The content guidelines provide clear expectations for the type of content the influencer needs to produce. This includes specifics like the number of posts required, post formats, necessary hashtags, mentions, and links to incorporate.

For our sunglasses campaign, the content expectations are:

- Two sponsored posts per platform (4 total)
- One Instagram photo post featuring sunglasses
- One Instagram Reels video wearing sunglasses
- One TikTok unboxing video
- One TikTok video showcasing sunglasses look
- Use campaign hashtag #SummerFunGiveaway
- Mention @brandsunglasses in 1 post per platform
- Include affiliate link in the bio

Providing detailed content guidelines gives the influencer a template for the exact type of posts needed to meet campaign objectives. They will know how many posts are required, which formats to use, and how to incorporate relevant hashtags, mentions and links. Specifying these parameters sets clear expectations for both parties.

TIMELINE

The timeline outlines key dates associated with content creation, review, and publishing. This keeps the campaign activities moving forward and on schedule. For our sunglasses campaign, the timeline is:

- Creative brief sent to influencer: June 1
- Influencer sends draft content for review: June 15
- Brand reviews and approves content: June 22
- Influencer publishes 1st IG photo post: July 1
- Influencer publishes 1st TikTok unboxing video: July 8
- Influencer publishes 1st IG reel: July 15
- Influencer publishes 2nd TikTok video: July 29

Having clear delivery dates for the influencer to submit drafts for approval ensures adequate lead time for review. And assigning publishing dates for the approved content keeps the social posts rolling out strategically over the campaign period. This timeline gives structure to the campaign and helps monitor progress for both parties.

COMPENSATION

The compensation section details how and when the influencer will be paid for their work on the branded campaign. For our sunglasses campaign, compensation will be:

- $500 per sponsored social media post
- Paid via PayPal or Venmo within 30 days of publishing approved content
- Additionally, the influencer will receive a gifted product of 3 pairs of sunglasses from our summer line

Outlining payment information, including amount, method, and timeline sets clear expectations around compensation. This enables the influencer to understand what they will receive in exchange for their partnership on the campaign.

MEASUREMENT

The measurement section outlines the key performance indicators (KPIs) and success metrics that will define how the brand evaluates campaign results. Tracking performance against these benchmarks will determine overall effectiveness. For our sunglasses campaign, we will measure:

- Sales using unique affiliate links and promo codes
- Engagement rate on sponsored posts
- Follower growth on Instagram and TikTok

- User-generated content usage and reach
- Brand awareness lift through surveys

By defining metrics like sales, engagement, reach, and awareness, we can closely monitor performance throughout the campaign and determine what resonates best with our target audience. Specifying clear success metrics and KPIs ensures the brand and influencer are aligned on what campaign results must be achieved. We'll go into more details about how to track the measurables in your campaign and show the return on investment (ROI) in Chapter 15.

CONTENT RIGHTS

The content rights section specifies how the brand can reuse and repurpose the content created through the influencer partnership. Defining these usage terms protects both parties. For this campaign, the brand will have the rights to:

- Share the content across the brand's own social media channels for promotional purposes
- Use the content in brand marketing materials like website, brochures, ads for up to one year from the date of publishing
- Edit or modify the content to better fit the brand guidelines and aesthetic
- Publicly attribute content to the influencer in relevant reposts or shares

The influencer retains ownership of the original content and can continue using it on their own channels. The brand cannot sell or profit from the content without additional permissions.

Clearly outlining content rights enables transparent expectations around how the brand can leverage the influencer's creative work. Both parties should review and agree to usage terms before campaign activation.

What You Learned

If you're not sure about everything that you need to do to build an influencer marketing campaign, let's take a minute to review what you read about in this chapter.

You need to write down your campaign objectives so that you know what you want to achieve in the campaign before you start. Work with your influencer to keep abreast of influencer marketing and industry trends so you have a better idea about how to reach your audience effectively. As part of that research, learn what the audience wants with your influencer to give your message a better chance of being heard.

An influencer marketing campaign brief is a critical document that outlines all the key details required for a successful brand-creator partnership. Taking the time to map out each element thoughtfully, from overview to goals to audience to content and more, ensures alignment and enables results.

With clear guidelines and expectations set through a comprehensive brief, the brand and influencer are empowered to create content that resonates with the target audience strategically. They can also effectively track performance against the defined success metrics.

Campaign briefs set the stage for truly impactful influencer marketing by providing a detailed roadmap for the collaboration. The transparency and clarity they establish builds a strong foundation where all parties can work together toward shared objectives.

Do you feel confident that you have a great campaign? Then let's continue on to Chapter 11 where we discuss running a campaign successfully.

Run a Successful Campaign

Running an influencer marketing campaign, like all marketing campaigns, isn't easy. There are common challenges you may encounter as you run your campaign, and flexibility is key to keeping your stress levels low. We're here to cover what those challenges are and how to overcome them.

Balance Creativity and Guidelines

Influencers have their own style and voice, and you need to plan your campaign to account for this. On the one hand, it's important to follow the guidelines in your campaign plan, but on the other, you want the influencer to speak in their authentic style and voice because it's what attracts their audience.

You may also have issues with the influencer ad-libbing and doing something that may run against the guidelines, but you won't know that until the campaign is underway. That ad-libbing, though, may lead you to more sales than you expected. (Some of the most memorable movie lines weren't in the script.) If you're concerned about an ad-libbed line, ask the influencer what they were thinking about when they went off script. They may give you an insight you never thought of and reinforce the value of your partnership.

Communicate Often

Speaking of talking and listening, don't forget to communicate with influencers throughout the campaign process. Provide them with any necessary support, answer their questions, and address their concerns in a timely manner. When you keep the lines of communication open, you'll reduce the risk of unpleasant surprises, such as inconsistent messaging that confuses viewers, as well as being able to adapt the campaign to better reach your audience.

When you don't communicate, prepare to waste your time and money. A client of Stephanie's, an organic baby food company, hired an influencer to do a live shopping event and planned their highly anticipated live shopping event for months. As the day grew closer, the excitement among the small business owners was palpable. They had worked tirelessly to create a memorable experience for their customers and were ready to introduce their delicious products to the world.

However, there was one crucial piece missing from their puzzle: a macro influencer to join them on this extraordinary journey. After an extensive search, they finally found the perfect influencer, known for her vibrant personality and massive following in the parenting community.

The influencer seemed like the missing link that would align the company with its target audience of eco-conscious moms and dads. The team knew that having her on board would skyrocket their brand's visibility and sales.

Speaking of talking and listening, the brand knew the importance of maintaining open lines of communication with influencers throughout the campaign. They understood that providing support, answering questions, and addressing concerns were vital in ensuring a successful event.

Unfortunately, the influencer's absence leading up to the event created a tsunami of chaos. The team spent hours upon hours and invested thousands of dollars preparing for the forty-five-minute shopping segment. As the clock ticked closer to the livestream, the influencer was nowhere to be found.

With beads of sweat forming on their foreheads, the team felt their excitement mutate into panic. All their efforts were at risk of going down the drain. The influencer finally arrived, but it was mere moments before the livestream was scheduled to begin. She appeared disheveled and unprepared as if she had not taken the time to understand the client's brand or products.

The once-charted course of success was now a rocky and uncertain path. The influencer rushed through the entire show in ten minutes, confusing the team and the audience. The dream collaboration had turned into a nightmare. The business owners were left with a bitter taste, having wasted time and money on a campaign that fell way below their expectations.

The moral of this story is that all business owners

> **TIP**
>
> Working with influencers can be tricky because they're used to doing things their way, and they may still do that even after you agree on what to do before the campaign starts. If you don't think you can be very diplomatic, you may want to find someone who can help with influencer relations. No matter what, being open and honest with your influencer may help them listen to your side of the story.

know about the importance of communication and preparation when working with influencers. As the brand reflected on its experience, it realized that it had unknowingly set itself up for failure by neglecting consistent communication with the influencer.

Adapt to Change

Social media platform algorithms and rules are constantly evolving, and a change can impact the reach and visibility of influencer content—perhaps dramatically. You need to constantly monitor changes in social media disclosure guidelines such as the FTC guidelines we talked about in Chapter 7, algorithm updates, or platform policies and adapt accordingly. If you don't, you and your team may be confused that you're not reaching as many people as you expected.

Negative Publicity

With any influencer marketing campaign, there is a risk of negative publicity or influencer controversies that can impact the success of your campaign. Despite your due diligence when you research influencers, you may be blindsided by hidden scandals, mistakes, and/or public backlash that not only harm their reputation but your brand's association with them.

In Chapter 6, we talked about including language in your agreement that specifies what behaviors can cause the agreement to be severed before its natural end date. That will keep your stress levels down, which is worth it even though you'll have to start over by finding another influencer.

Evaluate and Optimize

During and after the campaign, analyze the campaign results and evaluate its impact on your business, the influencer, and your audience. Talk with your team and the influencer about what worked well and areas for improvement. Use these insights to refine your strategies and make your next influencer campaign more effective.

What You Learned

You've reached the end of this chapter, so it's time to review what you learned about running a successful campaign.

It's important to balance the creativity of your influencer with the guidelines you have for the campaign. Social media platforms are constantly changing their algorithms and their rules, and you need to stay on top of those so you can adapt and ensure your campaign can still meet its objectives. Another wild card is unforeseen negative publicity that arises from something the influencer says or did in the past that harms the influencer and, by extension, your brand.

You also need to monitor the results of your campaign as you go along, adapt your strategy as needed, and then review the campaign's performance after the campaign has ended. Understanding what worked and what didn't will help make your next campaign stronger.

Another important factor to consider is leveraging paid social media, such as Google Ads and Facebook Ads, to keep your customers interested in your brand during and after the influencer campaign is over. Continue on to Chapter 12 to learn more.

Leverage Paid Social Media

The best way to rapidly grow an online audience and keep your brand top of mind and tip of tongue before, during, and after your influencer campaign is through paid advertising. In this chapter, you will learn which social media networks support advertising and how to handle creating your first campaign.

Between your website, hosting, and a few other tools (like Easil or Agorapulse), if you haven't yet dipped your toe into online advertising, you're probably spending $100 or less per month on marketing. Assuming you're willing to create content and manage your social media yourself, you should be able to invest some money into paid advertising.

While there are many options, like banner ads, Fiverr campaigns, and so on, in our experience, you'll get the best return with Google Ads and Facebook Ads. Depending on your business and target audience, you might also consider ads on X (formerly known as Twitter), Pinterest, and/or LinkedIn. Those three tend to have a higher *cost per click* (CPC), however, so let's focus on Google and Facebook initially. (We'll explain why we're including non-social advertising with Google in a moment.)

Google Ads

When you decide to advertise with Google, you have a lot of options, but we'll give you a high-level perspective here so you can decide if it's interesting to you.

Using Google Ads, you can place advertisements above or near search results that are relevant to your business and brand. Because the audience is people who are actively searching on a particular topic or keyword, we refer to this as *search intent*. You don't have to guess whether they're interested in that topic—they are.

Additionally, Google serves ads on actual websites, so you can place your ads in its "Display Network" and reach people who are, perhaps, reading about a topic but not necessarily searching for it on Google. The sites in the Display Network have signed up for Google's AdSense program; they earn a commission for every ad view and click.

When you place ads with Google, you set a bid amount and a daily budget. The *bid amount* is the maximum amount you're willing to spend per click (e.g., 25 cents), and your ad then competes against other advertisers interested in reaching the same audience. Ads with higher bids are displayed first on each page of search results, or more often on content sites within the Display Network.

Again, you're only charged when someone clicks on your ad, so you'll want to find a balance between ranking high for your ad and getting enough clicks, leads, and sales to make it worthwhile.

Your ads will continue to display until you reach your daily budget limit and then stop automatically, so it's up to you how much you spend.

Facebook Ads

When you decide to advertise with Facebook, you can either create a new ad or use a status update you've already shared.

The ad fee structure is similar to Google in that you can set a daily budget, but you don't set a bid per click. Instead, Facebook will begin showing your ads; the more interest people show, the less per click you'll be charged. So it's in everyone's best interests to create Facebook ad posts that are interesting and compelling.

In addition to driving traffic, you can use Facebook ads for brand awareness and simply pay for *engagement*—in other words, likes, comments, and shares. The more people engage with your ad and post, the more likely it is to be seen by people outside your target audience.

Unlike Google search ads, which are 100 percent text, Facebook ads can be links, images, or even video. You can use a single image or a carousel of images. You can even upload multiple images and let Facebook test which one resonates best with your audience.

You can also set up a *remarketing pixel* (a snippet of code installed on your website) so that Facebook can track users who have been to your site and allow you to "remarket" to them with an ad specifically targeting them. Let's explore this concept further.

The Power of Search + Remarketing

Here's how remarketing works. Once you have a Facebook pixel installed on your site and are driving targeted traffic using Google Ads (and, of course, other means), you are equipped to amplify the *frequency illusion*.

Have you ever noticed that the day after you drive a new car off the lot, it seems like everyone else around you suddenly owns the same car? Don't worry—it's not a conspiracy. It's actually an illusion—a misperception that plays out in our minds due to a new or renewed awareness of something.

That's the frequency illusion (aka, the Baader-Meinhof phenomenon), and brands that successfully pursue video content as part of their social media strategy are uniquely positioned to leverage this phenomenon. With a pixel in place, you can now create Facebook ads targeting people who have visited your site, or even specific pages or posts within your site. This is referred to as retargeting or remarketing.

You've doubtless experienced this yourself. Spend a couple of minutes looking at cars on Infiniti.com, and suddenly every site you go to is displaying Infiniti ads. Because you showed interest in a brand or product by visiting their site, advertisers smartly wish to capitalize on that interest and keep themselves top of mind.

You can now do exactly the same thing!

When your Google ads effectively capture someone as they're searching for you or information you have published, they register as a visitor with the Facebook pixel. If Facebook recognizes them as a user *and* you are running a remarketing campaign that includes someone like them, you can layer brand-awareness or added-benefit advertising on Facebook or Instagram, which will potentially be seen by someone who was already demonstrating search intent *and* is familiar with your brand. This is extraordinarily powerful and effective.

Couple this technique with problem-solving content, and you now have a means to reach people who you know have an issue and may need help to solve it. That help might include:

- How-to guides
- Answers to frequently asked questions
- Case studies

Let's say you're a local attorney specializing in family law. You can write a series of blog posts that answer common questions about divorce, child custody, estate planning, and so on, and then use Google Ads to help people who are searching for those answers find your content. You can then place Facebook ads that encourage those people to call you for more information and assistance.

Or let's imagine you own a wedding dress shop. Same scenario: Create content that answers common questions brides have about their special day, use Google Ads to drive intentional traffic, and then leverage Facebook to make sure those brides know about your gorgeous dresses by placing ads showcasing your latest offerings and retargeting your website traffic.

Whatever products or services you have to offer, this technique can be implemented, tested, refined, and then scaled up.

Other Platforms

As we mentioned earlier, Facebook isn't the only option when it comes to social advertising. It's worth taking a moment to consider and even test each of the other networks, particularly if that platform and predominant audience suit your business.

INSTAGRAM

You may already know that since Instagram is owned by Facebook, advertising on Instagram is handled within the Facebook Ads Manager. Ads are similarly structured, and campaigns that you launch on Facebook can also include Instagram.

So why didn't we just include Instagram in the previous section?

First, it is a separate platform, which means your audience and results will be very different from Facebook. The demographics of Instagram users tend to skew younger than Facebook's, for instance.

Second, Instagram's aesthetic is one of square images and video, with short captions and hashtags. While it's possible for Facebook advertising assets to look good on Instagram, it's more likely that you will need to revise your ads before they run there.

When crafting an ad campaign in Facebook Ads Manager, you build the ad and select your destinations. You can then preview how the ad will look on Facebook vs. Instagram, mobile vs. desktop, and so on. Always check those previews, and if the ad does not render beautifully on all platforms, take a moment to create a separate campaign with alternative assets.

Third, realize that people on Instagram do not expect to click on outside links. Since standard image and video posts cannot have working links, people are accustomed to simply scrolling through their Instagram feeds. Ads, however, can include links, which appear as a Learn More bar across the bottom of the ad.

So, an ad link that might get a decent clickthrough rate on Facebook may not perform as well on Instagram. Consider carefully what you hope to achieve with the Instagram ad, and choose the imagery and copy you need to elicit that behavior. While organic referral traffic from Instagram is still poor, ad-driven and ecommerce referral traffic is increasing exponentially for that network.

At the end of the day, realize that Instagram will likely be your poorest driver of traffic. Granted, anyone who does tap on an Instagram-promoted link is likely very interested in learning more about what you're promoting. But most people will just keep scrolling.

X, FORMERLY KNOWN AS TWITTER

There are several different kinds of ads you can run on X, each with different benefits and mechanisms.

First, just like Facebook and Instagram, you can choose to create an ad from scratch within the advertising dashboard, or you can promote an existing tweet. In fact, when creating a campaign in X, you can choose to include multiple tweets within that campaign.

Suppose you have published an ebook and have already posted several tweets about it, each including a link to a landing page that offers it to new subscribers. You could bundle all those tweets into a campaign that promotes and amplifies each tweet accordingly.

One significant difference in terms of ad placement is that X gives you the option of promoting a tweet into someone's feed depending on who they are, who they're following, or what they're searching on. Let's break that down.

Because X doesn't use extensive research about sections, nor does it have pages to follow or groups to join, the amount of personal information it can collect about its users is quite minimal. Therefore, while there are some limited targeting options, such as basic demographics and interests, that's not what Twitter wants you to focus on.

Instead, you would target your followers, followers of other accounts, and look-alike audiences based on those other accounts. Obviously, it helps at this point to have a good understanding of your industry and the top X profiles your target audience may be interested in.

This might include competitors, educational organizations, and sources of industry news.

The assumption is that because someone is following X (no pun intended), they must therefore be interested in Y, and may possibly click to learn more about Z. If this sounds tricky and unreliable, that's because it is.

A more effective form of targeting hearkens back to how we approached Google: search intent. But what do people search for on X? Hashtags and keywords.

When crafting your promotional campaign, you can choose to target specific keywords or keyword phrases, and when your audience searches for those, your promoted tweet will appear at the top of the results. Neat, huh?

What's notable about X campaigns is that you can combine follower targeting and keyword targeting for a really interesting mix of opportunities to get your tweet content in front of your desired audience.

You can, of course, promote your profile if you'd like to use ad dollars to reach and grow your audience. You can even allow X to automatically promote your channel's content, a service that has been dubbed "X Promote Mode." The platform says, "On average, accounts will reach 30,000 additional people and add 30 followers each month." It costs a flat $99 per month and isn't a bad idea for new or relatively new accounts.

LINKEDIN

For years, LinkedIn has been relatively ignored by marketers and advertisers due to the limiting belief that it was only for professionals seeking employment and networking.

All that is true, of course, but LinkedIn is so much more than that today.

With the addition of LinkedIn Live video, users can connect in a far more relatable way. It has also become a very viable publishing platform, resulting in higher *and* longer usage—both elements of user behavior that are essential to successful advertising.

What's unique about LinkedIn is the high degree of targeting granularity you can achieve. Consider job titles, for instance. On Facebook, users may or may not enter their job title or keep it updated as their role changes. On LinkedIn, however, most will make sure that and other key elements of their profile are up-to-date and complete.

This means if you want to target CMOs with your advertising because you have a marketing automation tool they might be interested in, you can easily find them on LinkedIn.

Most other elements of advertising on LinkedIn are similar to other platforms. You create campaigns and campaign groups and ads within those to maintain structure and organization. The ads themselves can be images or videos with links, and they can be limited and targeted to specific locations or other demographics.

One important note: Advertising on LinkedIn is still the most expensive of all social media platforms. You can expect to spend several dollars per click on average, and therefore the minimum daily budget for any campaign is $10. However, if you're able to place lucrative offers in front of a highly segmented and interested audience, you have a high likelihood of success.

PINTEREST

Pinterest advertising is currently segmented into six types of campaigns:

1. Awareness
2. Traffic
3. App install
4. Shopping
5. Conversions
6. Video views

Most of these are similar to the ads on other social media platforms like Facebook. Using ads to build awareness or drive traffic makes sense. It's interesting that Pinterest has separate campaigns for app installs and video views. But shopping and conversions campaigns are where Pinterest can be of real benefit.

Shopping, of course, has to do with product sales, so if you're selling items through your website this is a very viable campaign objective.

When Pinterest says "conversions," they're specifically referring to nonpurchase conversions such as subscriptions or downloads.

The beauty of having these varied campaign objectives to choose from is that any campaign you set up will be optimized to achieve that objective. That means the cost of the campaign will be optimized as well. While ads on other platforms can drive traffic to a product, and can even measure the resulting conversions, they're less able to algorithmically benefit from those sales and generate more.

When creating Pinterest campaigns, you should install the Pinterest pixel on your site (just like on Facebook, Twitter, and LinkedIn). Not only will that allow you to measure the results of your ads post-click, but it will also help you target website visitors through remarketing, as we discussed earlier.

As you start to create your campaign, you will see a variety of initial audiences to add, including:

- Engaged pinners (people who have engaged with your Pinterest pins)
- Lookalike pinners (a larger audience based on your own pinners)
- Website visitors

Depending on the type of campaign you select, you will have more options to select from next, such as Product Category, Interests, or Keywords.

With Interests, unfortunately, you're restricted to Pinterest's somewhat limited set, which is based on what typical Pinterest users are pinning. These categories may have nothing to do with your business, but they include:

- Animals
- Architecture
- Art
- Beauty
- Children's fashion
- Design
- DIY and crafts
- Education
- Electronics
- Entertainment
- Event planning
- Finance
- Food and drinks
- Gardening
- Health
- Home decor

- Men's fashion
- Parenting
- Quotes
- Sport
- Travel
- Vehicles
- Wedding
- Women's fashion

If you aren't a heavy Pinterest user yourself, this list (each of which has several sub-categories to choose from) should be very telling. Pinterest generally attracts people who are planning or dreaming, so whether it's recipes, clothes, travel destinations, or home improvement projects, that's how most people search and use Pinterest. If your business or pin content falls within one of those interests, drill down and select the most appropriate category. If not, skip that section.

Keywords, on the other hand, are where any brand can leverage user behavior, history, and, most important, intent. Just like with Twitter, you can target keywords on Pinterest and capture user intent when they're actually searching for the information or solution you offer. And Pinterest makes this exceedingly easy.

In the Keyword area of campaign creation, type in a short keyword or phrase to the right, and below that Pinterest will automatically populate it with actual searches by users, as well the search volume. You can then choose from suggested keywords and make sure there's adequate monthly volume to make advertising worthwhile.

As you add keywords, they'll appear in your growing list to the left. Pinterest recommends a minimum of 25 keywords to target, so keep plugging in ideas and selecting recommendations until you have at least that many.

There are minimal demographic options to select, such as gender or age, and unfortunately you can only advertise within the United States.

You may select a daily or lifetime budget, and then either create new pins or choose from existing pins to promote. Once you've done that, you're ready to launch your first campaign!

YOUTUBE

As you know, YouTube is all about videos, so unsurprisingly, ads must be in video format as well. You must upload the video you choose for your ad to your YouTube channel, but it can be private or unlisted if you do not wish for people to view it organically.

YouTube ads can run at the beginning of other people's videos (pre-roll) or during their videos (in-stream). The videos on which your ads play are determined either by topic or channel, along with standard demographic filters that you choose when creating the ad. You can select very specific criteria, such as a particular channel, or choose broad criteria and allow YouTube's algorithm to place your ad accordingly.

YouTube, which is owned by Google, uses Google Ads to manage ad campaigns and preferences. So, if you've run Google ads in the past, a lot about YouTube advertising will seem familiar. But unlike Google ads, which are charged per click, YouTube ads are charged per view.

And they are extremely affordable! Brands can leverage YouTube ads to generate thousands of ad views for as little as $1 a day.

But keep in mind, viewers can skip most ads after a few seconds, and even if they watch the entire ad, they are unlikely to take immediate action. YouTube ads are best used for brand awareness, similar to TV commercials.

A lot will depend on your brand, what you're advertising, and the videos on which that ad appears. Try to imagine your viewer's frame of mind—is it likely they will see your ad and be willing to tap to learn more immediately? If not, make sure that the video makes a lasting impression and serves to accomplish brand lift.

An example that's easy to relate to even if you don't use YouTube would be Super Bowl commercials. No advertiser expects to persuade you to get up and go to the store in the middle of the year's biggest football game. What they hope is to make an impression that lasts long enough for you to make that purchase at the next opportunity.

Walmart ran a brilliant ad (which you can easily find online) showing famous sci-fi characters using its grocery pickup, which has resulted in numerous publications making reference to the bit. This has resulted in far more additional views and immeasurable brand lift.

OTHER NETWORKS

There are many smaller social networks you can advertise on, including some that are extremely popular in different countries or for specific demographic groups. TikTok, Snapchat, and Twitch, for instance, all support ads. You can even use Facebook Ads Manager to target the Messenger and WhatsApp platforms.

The point is that if your target audience prefers a specific platform, and we haven't already discussed it here, do a little digging and see if they offer advertising solutions. They won't make it hard to find—typically a Google search for "[network name] ads" will result in a direct link to their advertising page. If they don't now, they soon will. Social networks by their very nature are free to users and therefore must implement a monetization strategy of some kind if they want to survive. Advertising is the model that has been proved to work.

What You Learned

Now that you've come to the end of this chapter, it's time to recap what you learned about leveraging paid social media.

The appeal of paid social media advertising is twofold: It's affordable and measurable. Regardless of which platform you choose to invest in, it's far more affordable than traditional advertising, and you can track exactly what you received from each dollar you spend—right down to your bottom-line business results.

That means with paid social advertising you have something of a marketing unicorn: true determination of ROI! With paid social ads, you can grow your following, reach new audiences, and of course drive traffic and conversions.

The purpose of this chapter was to give you a solid understanding of what each platform is capable of. Better yet, with all the content you've created for your social media and influencer marketing campaigns, you can repurpose that content for other channels. You can read all about it in Chapter 13.

Repurpose and Reuse Social Content

In this chapter, we're going to talk about how to turn social media activity into valuable website content, or content for other channels.

Specifically, we'll cover five different techniques that you can pick and choose from, or even use them all! Coupled with articles you write to help educate your audience, these techniques can fuel your blog and drive your content marketing efforts indefinitely.

And yet blog posts, while low-cost, can still seem high-risk. You can spend hours, sometimes days, slaving over an article, only to publish it and watch it sink without a ripple of response.

Was it that poorly written? Or was it simply on a subject your audience had no interest in?

In this chapter, we're not just going to talk about how you can save time by turning social media content into website content; we'll also show you how careful selection of content mitigates risk.

Let's say you have a Facebook post that went viral and a tweet that got no engagement whatsoever. Which do you think will perform better as part of a blog post?

The viral one, of course!

While there are many reasons one social post might outperform another, the one reason we can reliably count on when creating subsequent pieces of content is the topic.

As we go through the following five techniques, please bear that in mind. When you have a choice, always select from the most successful social posts and use the native engagement indicators, such as likes and shares, to guide you.

Technique 1: Live Video

This is perhaps our favorite technique, because you can use the video in your influencer marketing campaign on the influencer's primary channel. What's more, you can integrate the influencer marketing video in other company videos on other platforms. When you get questions and comments about your influencer's video, you can use that material as the basis for a follow-up video that addresses those issues.

Whether you livestream on Facebook, YouTube, LinkedIn, Instagram, or some other platform, live video is an opportunity for you to showcase your brand, collaborate with influencers, and engage with a live audience.

If it were simply recorded video of you sharing your thoughts, it would be little different from a blog post—just in a different medium. Live video, however, has additional aspects and benefits.

For one thing, since you can broadcast with other people on most social media platforms, you can bring guests and experts into your video who will help you create the content. Instead of relying solely on your own expertise, you can capitalize on the depth of knowledge these guests possess, whether it's a live discussion, interview, or Q&A.

Additionally, the fact that you have a live audience can actually help you create content. Throughout the broadcast, you can read comments left by viewers and bring those comments into the broadcast as questions to be answered.

In fact, some brands and broadcasters devote an entire broadcast to answering audience questions; the video is entirely unscripted and requires very little preparation as a result.

Once your video is over, that's when the real magic happens. Let's assume that you have decided to broadcast to Facebook using an app like Ecamm or StreamYard so you can bring in guests easily. You've spent thirty minutes interviewing an expert in your industry, and now the broadcast is done.

You now have a thirty-minute video that you can download as an MP4 file. At an average speaking rate of 150 words per minute, that video can be transcribed into roughly a 4,500-word blog post! If the average blog post is 750 words, and blog posts that are 2,000-plus words perform best, how well do you think a 4,500-word blog post is going to do?

Stephanie put repurposing techniques to good use in 2023 when she hosted Showrunner Secrets from the Set, a series of five livestream videos in partnership with Ecamm that she then published on YouTube. (youtube.com/playlist?list=PL44QjsM_d1tDWwjJgoRwuf8uuraJkZKRl)

After the series ended, Stephanie repurposed the video into a series of blog posts on the Ecamm website (ecamm.com/blog/tag/showrunner/) and then turned those blog posts into an ebook titled *Leap Into Live Selling Digital Guidebook* that now sells for $35 on the Ecamm website. (ecamm.ck.page/products/leap-into-live-selling-digital-guide)

However, if you're sticking to your original principle of only using successful social posts, that means that before you transcribe and publish this video as a blog post, make sure it was a good video. Were there more viewers than usual? Were there great comments and discussion? Did you and your guests engage in a lively debate? Whatever your barometer for success is, make sure it applies before you take this extra step.

Once you have the transcript (and inexpensive transcription services like Descript, Rev.com, and Quicc.io are available to help with that), you can publish it as a blog post with just a brief introduction explaining what people are about to read.

Stephanie also put together a tutorial about how to re-purpose your livestream at lightscameralive.com/blog/how-to-use-descript-to-repurpose-your-livestream.

You can also embed the original video along with your post, which serves two purposes:

1. Visitors to the blog may prefer to watch the video rather than read the post, which adds 30 minutes to their time on the site.
2. Anyone who engages with the video by liking or commenting on it will create a story in their feed for their friends to see.

There are even more possibilities. You can strip the audio track from the video and turn that into a separate podcast. If you pull short segments of the audio into an app like Headliner, you can create audiograms—basically video files that use a static image with an audio track. You can slice out specific segments of the video and use them for social posts or as the basis for additional blog posts.

Suppose, for instance, that you and your expert talked about a specific topic for five minutes and answered a couple of viewer questions. That segment alone is probably valuable enough to upload separately to Facebook or YouTube. And de-pending on the topic, it might be worth expanding on it in an article of its own. Finally, take note of any specific comments your guests make that are truly brilliant and turn those into quotes or even quote graphics that, again, you can use within blog posts or other social media stories. For example, Opus Clip (https://www.opus.pro/) uses AI to identify short-form videos from your livestream. Opus Clip also reports which videos are more likely to go viral. So, if the brand does an interview with a guest, the brand can then tag and invite the guest as a collaborator on Instagram so that the short-form video gets more reach.

> **TIP**
>
> Working with influencers can be tricky because they're used to doing things their way, and they may still do that even after you agree on what to do before the campaign starts. If you don't think you can be very diplomatic, you may want to find someone who can help with influencer relations. No matter what, being open and honest with your influencer may help your influencer listen to your side of the story.

Technique 2: User-Generated Content

While the first technique relied on video content that you created yourself, this technique gets to use posts that you had nothing to do with.

Posts that other people create, which we then use for our own business, are called user-generated content. While it's most often used in reference to content other people create about our business, such as video testimonials, it doesn't have to be limited to that.

One popular example these days is news articles about a trending topic that consist mostly of tweets from other people about that topic: "So-and-so did something stupid and the internet has gone crazy about it." The story has one or two paragraphs about the actual event and then half a dozen tweets from random people sharing their opinions.

That technique might work very well if you work in an industry in which there are often big news events on which people are commenting publicly. Send a quick direct message asking for permission to use their tweet in a story, grab the embed code Twitter provides, and you have a nice blog post.

But what if nothing much newsworthy happens in your industry?

There's nothing wrong with using posts that really are about your business in some way, even if they aren't news, so watch for those. Also watch for great comments on your other blog posts or social posts.

You could also look for blog posts and articles written by others and reference or curate those. For instance, suppose someone writes a blog about the "10 Best Providers of Widgets" and names your business in that list. You could summarize and link to that article in a blog post of your own.

The point is to always be on the lookout for content that other people create on their own sites, in your blog comments, or on social networks that's either directly about your business or about your industry in general, and think about how you might use it. Using content generated by other users and customers is a great way to make connections with them and the rest of your target audience.

Technique 3: Embedded Social Media Posts

In the first technique, we mentioned you can embed the recorded video from Facebook or YouTube into a blog post with the video's transcript. In the second technique, we talked about how to embed tweets or other social posts from other people into a blog to help create a story. How else might we use and embed social posts?

First, social media posts make great examples, even if you're not talking about the post itself. We'll explain.

Let's say you're a business that provides a service to people that you can take pictures of, whether it's cutting hair, building decks, or something else.

Now, you could write a blog post about a particular project and just embed the pictures into that article. But why not leverage the power of social media instead? Post the pictures to your Facebook Page before you publish your article and then embed the Facebook post into your blog post.

Just like with embedded videos, any kind of embedded social post will benefit from the additional views and engagement it receives from your blog readers.

In fact, there's nothing stopping you from using this technique on older content as well. Let's say you have an article from a couple of years ago that still gets good search engine traffic. Take a few moments to update that article and embed a relevant Facebook video or photo album, and watch as those social posts get renewed interest from your organic traffic.

Another way to use this technique is to use social media to poll or survey your audience and then embed that post into an article that talks about the topic and shares the results of the poll. We'll come back to this idea in Technique 5.

Technique 4: Turn Discussions Into Blog Posts

While turning live video into blog content might be our favorite technique, turning discussions into blog posts might be the one we've had the most long-term success with.

How often have you commented on a Facebook or Instagram post, or participated in a discussion on X? All the time, right? Real, back-and-forth conversation is what social networks are designed for.

Now, if you're like us, a lot of those discussions have been professional, as many of our social connections are peers and colleagues. We'll talk about what's happening with Instagram shadow bans, or what's going to happen to third-party video tools when Facebook finishes integrating all the needed functions with Creator Studio. We also talk to other business owners and readers who want to know about something in our niche, and we answer their questions.

While doing all this, we have trained ourselves to automatically think about a potential blog post whenever we find ourselves spending more than a couple of minutes on an answer. If one person on Facebook wants to know about something relating to your business or industry, there are likely many other people who want to know that same information.

In those instances, we've found the best option is to post our comment and conclude the discussion, and then copy and paste all the relevant text into an Evernote note. That way we can easily find it later and decide whether it would really make for a good blog post.

Technique 5: Ask Questions

Finally, the one technique that we see far too few bloggers and marketers use is to *ask questions!* Just *ask* your audience what they want to know about!

As long as you've been making even the slightest effort to have real conversations with your growing audience, some of your followers will have questions.

Sometimes they'll be quick questions you can answer in a brief comment. Sometimes they'll be questions you've already answered, which is a perfect opportunity to share a link to an article and impress them with your expertise.

Sometimes they'll be questions you haven't answered that require a little space to address. Those are perfect subjects for videos or blog posts! And not only are those questions the source of blog content, but you can also embed the original social post within the blog, as we described in Technique 3 above.

The beauty of this technique is twofold. First, you don't have to worry about not getting enough questions. Most of us only have enough time to create new articles two to four times a month, so one or two great questions once in a while is fabulous!

Second, since someone else asked the question, you know there's at least one person interested in the answer! Too often our ideas for blog posts are spun out of the void between our ears, which means we're gambling with our time, just like Touchstone Pictures did with *The 13th Warrior.*

Your time is one of your most valuable commodities. You don't want to squander it creating content that no one cares about. When you begin to leverage all the types of social media content available to you, you can mitigate that risk and even create terrific synergies between your blog and social media.

What You Learned

We've reached the end of this chapter, so let's summarize what you read about repurposing and reusing social content. There are five different techniques you can use to get the most out of your content. The first, and our favorite, is video. If your influencer uses video primarily in your campaign, you can place snippets of that video that promotes the product and/or service into your own videos.

You can connect with user-generated content, such as comments and questions generated by your influencer marketing campaign. Other sources of content to reuse include embedding social media posts into other platforms, turning discussions into blog posts, and going the direct route and asking questions of your audience.

Once you feel satisfied with repurposing your content to get the most from your influencer marketing campaign, it's time to measure your results. An integral measurement of your campaign is how many new leads you received so you can turn as many of them into sales. Chapter 14 discusses how to turn those leads into customers.

Manage Your Leads

An integral part of your influencer marketing campaign is to capture leads that you can convert into customers sooner or later. You need to set up a streamlined process to capture lead information during the campaign building process because you won't be able to profit from it, let alone know how well your campaign is doing. You can do this by using lead capture forms on your website that people can link to from the influencer's social media channel. You may also want to have a dedicated landing page on your site just for the influencer campaign.

At a minimum, you should collect their names and email addresses, but there may be additional details such as what product is of most interest to them.

As you may have suspected, there's more to do when you collect leads from an influencer marketing campaign. Here are things you should think about setting up before your campaign starts.

> **TIP**
>
> No matter what data you decide to collect, you need to implement opt-in mechanisms to have people who sign up give their consent in the form. Otherwise, you will run afoul of state and federal spam laws that people will call you on, and it will damage or destroy your campaign and leave you open to legal issues.

Align with Your Sales Team

This may seem obvious when you've set up other types of marketing campaigns, but you need to collaborate closely with your sales team before you launch your influencer marketing campaign. Even if you already have a sales system set up to manage lead generation, this is a good opportunity to review your system and ensure that it (and your team) can handle the increased number of leads, as well as how marketing and sales should communicate during the campaign.

Automate Lead Management Processes

When you align your campaign with the sales team, it's a good time to check and see if your marketing automation tools are up to the task. If you don't have tools implemented, you should do so before the campaign starts. Those tools include automated email workflows, lead scoring systems, and notifications. Your sales team and your influencer may have suggestions for you—and they'll probably be on your side when you make your case to the powers that be.

Build Tracking Mechanisms

As you build your influencer campaign, implement trackable elements such as a unique URL for the marketing campaign, promo codes, and a landing page, don't forget to use your analytics tools and customer relationship management (CRM) systems to track and monitor your leads. If you don't have them, this is a great time to get them. If you're working with an influencer who has done marketing campaigns, they may be able to work with your sales and marketing teams to find the right fits for your business.

Qualify and Track Leads

As with all leads from any marketing campaign, not all leads are ready to convert right away. Before you launch your campaign, review your lead qualification processes so you can identify the leads that have the best conversion potential. You should continuously track interaction from your leads including email open rates, click-through rates to your website, website visits, and how many people submit your lead capture form.

If you don't have a scoring system, an influencer marketing campaign is a good time to implement one because as with any lead, following up quickly is important. Email responses are quick and easy when you have automated email workflows set up. You need to work with your sales team to find out what leads with what scores get a direct phone call from a sales rep and which ones just get follow-up content.

Provide Valuable Content

Speaking of content, you need to provide personalized, targeted content through your email marketing system, on your website, and on your social media profiles. There are many different forms of content you can share including an email newsletter, blog posts, videos, podcasts, guides and workbooks, and exclusive offers that align with their interests and needs.

As you continue providing information on a regular schedule—yet not so often that you overwhelm them and cause them to unsubscribe—you build your credibility and people see your business as a trusted resource they should do business with.

What You Learned

Now that we've reached the end of this chapter, take a minute or two to review what you learned about managing leads.

Effectively managing leads from your influencer marketing campaign requires you to coordinate with your sales team before you start. If you don't have lead management processes and tracking mechanisms in place, you need to put those systems in place before you start. If you do, then you and your sales team should agree that your systems can handle the influx as well as qualify and track your leads. With all your leads, you need to provide personalized, valuable content in a variety of media to build relationships with potential customers.

When you have leads from your influencer marketing campaign, you need to measure not only how many leads you have but the effectiveness of your campaign overall. Continue on to Chapter 15 to find out how to track every element of your campaign so you can prove the return on investment (ROI) to yourself and the powers that be.

Prove the ROI of Your Influencer Marketing

Proving the return on investment (ROI) of an influencer marketing campaign is challenging because social media is complex and there are multiple variables to track. That doesn't mean finding ROI is only meant for alchemists. You can take several approaches to show the social media ROI of your influencer marketing campaign to your influencer, your sales and marketing teams, any higher-ups in your company, and yourself.

Set Clear Goals and Objectives

First, let us remind you about what we discussed in earlier chapters: Before launching your influencer campaign, define specific and measurable goals that align with your objectives for the campaign. Here are some goals you should think about implementing for your campaign:

- Increased brand awareness
- Increased website traffic
- More leads generated
- More conversions from leads to customers
- Higher sales

In sum, without clear goals, you won't have benchmarks for measuring ROI.

Track and Measure Key Metrics

As we noted in earlier chapters, you can't know how you're meeting your goals unless you use tools and analytics that help you measure the performance of your campaign. If you don't have a metrics tracker already, your sales and marketing teams are probably clamoring for you to implement one.

What metrics do you need to track? Here's a list to review so you can pick and choose the metrics that fit your goals:

- Reach
- Impressions
- Engagements including likes, comments, and shares
- Website clicks
- The conversation rate from leads to customers
- Sales revenue from the campaign

> **TIP**
>
> You may also want to talk with your influencer about tools and analytics, because chances are that they've worked on other campaigns before and have an idea of what works (and what doesn't).

Know Your Key Performance Indicators

You may have heard of KPIs, which is an acronym for key performance indicators. And you may have guessed that KPIs are vital to understanding how a marketing campaign performs. In the case of influencer marketing, there are five KPIs you need to track.

START WITH A HANDY SPREADSHEET

We talked about the SARAL influencer marketing platform earlier in this book, and they have a free Influencer Program KPI Reporting Sheet in Google Sheets that's a template for tracking your activity over a period of sixteen weeks, though you can extend the time period. *(docs. google.com/spreadsheets/d/1HrjU5-UraTNSuLJF7vma_rFn_KX_haaxzm_0Ncs4j-k/ edit#gid=659533530)*

The spreadsheet has ten columns so you can enter information and share the progress with your team as well as the powers that be. The ten columns are:

- The niche and/or hashtags you use for the campaign.
- The number of emails and/or direct messages sent to influencers about the campaign.
- How many replies you received from influencers to your emails and/or direct messages.
- How many influencers you onboarded for your campaign(s).
- The target number of onboarded influencers you set before the campaign.
- If you followed up with the influencer in conversation.
- If you followed up with the influencer after activation.
- How many live posts the influencer made, such as a video or a post on their social media channels.

- The target number of live posts you set before the campaign.
- Your notes and what you learned from the campaign, such as what hashtags perform better with the audience.

REACH AND IMPRESSIONS

Reach and impressions are fundamental KPIs to assess your campaign's visibility and potential audience exposure. Tools like Google Analytics, social media analytics, and influencer marketing platforms like GRIN, Mavrck, and SARAL can provide insights into the reach and impressions generated by your influencers.

By tracking reach and impressions, you can determine the best time to publish your content, analyze how many people are viewing your content multiple times, and make data-driven decisions to improve your influencer marketing campaign.

These metrics are closely related to goals like brand awareness and audience-building, as they focus on getting as many eyes on your content as possible rather than persuading viewers to take a specific action, like making a purchase.

ENGAGEMENT METRICS

Engagement metrics, such as likes, comments, shares, and saves, offer valuable insights into how your audience engages with your content and how well your brand is being received. By tracking engagement metrics, you can determine how well your content strategy aligns with user interest, identify areas of improvement, and plan strategic campaigns to engage with users meaningfully.

For example, comments like this are what you're looking for: "Thank you for this. I've been searching for a product that can help with XYZ. Definitely going to check this out."

Hearing common pain points your product solves helps you address this in future marketing. Maybe you'll find a pain point or audience you haven't marketed to. Getting customers to talk and using their language in your copy is a gold mine!

Engagement is also a good indicator of how loyal your customers will be and how likely they are to buy, repeat purchases, and share your product or service with others.

REFERRAL TRAFFIC

While reach, impressions, and engagement are essential KPIs to track, it's equally important to consider the impact of influencer campaigns on referral traffic to external sources, like websites, social media channels, or sales pages.

By closely monitoring referral traffic, you get a close look into the success of your influencer campaigns beyond social media engagement. It provides a tangible link between your influencers' content and actual website visits, giving you a deeper understanding of the impact and ROI of your influencer marketing efforts.

There are two ways you can track and analyze this KPI.

UTM (Urchin Tracking Module) Parameters

Incorporate unique UTM parameters in the influencers' content links shared across different channels. UTM parameters are tags added to the URL, which allows you to track the traffic source and campaign details in Google Analytics or other web analytics tools.

Website Analytics

Regularly analyze your website analytics to identify the referral sources that drive the most traffic. Look for referral domains, such as social media platforms, blogs, or other websites where your influencers' content is being shared.

Remember, referral traffic is not only about quantity but also about quality. While high volumes of traffic are desirable, it's equally important to assess factors like bounce rate, time spent on site, and pages visited per session.

CONVERSION RATES AND SALES

Let's put our "Captain Obvious" hats on for a second: influencer campaigns should drive conversions and sales. If anyone asks why, give them these three good reasons:

- Tracking conversions provides tangible evidence that your campaign drives desired actions, such as purchases, sign-ups, or downloads. This data helps you assess their influencer collaborations' ROI and overall success.
- You can set up future campaigns for better success by identifying high-performing influencers, content types, or platforms that generate the most conversions. For example, you can see if your audience prefers Instagram over YouTube or if specific platforms drive higher-quality leads.
- Conversion tracking provides valuable insights into customer behavior and preferences. For example, identify popular items, product categories, or price points that resonate with your audience.

With a social media management tool like Agorapulse, you can see how organic social media content published by an influencer drove conversions.

AUDIENCE GROWTH

One of the key goals of influencer marketing is to reach and connect with a wider audience. The wider the audience, the better chance your reach and sales go up.

By monitoring the growth of your social media following, email subscribers, or website visitors, you can evaluate the success of your campaigns in attracting new audience members. It's a clear sign your message resonates and that the partnership with your influencer is a good match.

How do you track audience growth? Use native social media analytics, email marketing tools, and social media management platforms like Agorapulse to monitor the growth of your social media following.

By understanding the demographics and engagement of your expanding audience, you can optimize your influencer marketing strategies and ensure long-term success in reaching and connecting with new customers.

Use Sentiment Analysis

It can be hard to tell someone's emotions and tone in social media posts, online comments, and/or email message. Yes, we use emoji symbols and acronyms to help convey emotions, but these can also be misinterpreted. One common example is with the acronym LOL, where some people think it means "lots of love." They have to be reminded that it really means "laughing out loud" to explain why an online experience has become rather awkward.

Your company can't afford those kinds of misunderstandings, as they can not only drive potential customers away, but they can also prompt customers to tell their family and friends to stay away from your business. Companies are turning more toward AI and natural language processing in sentiment analysis tools.

These tools analyze text conversations and evaluate the emotion, intent, and tone in each message. A sentiment analysis tool saves your sales and marketing team valuable time by automatically processing your messages from various channels and tells you if that feedback is positive, negative, or neutral.

You can also track the sentiment over time to see if there are any sentiment shifts, positive or negative, during the life of your influencer marketing campaign. You can also use the data during a postmortem after the campaign to see what your audience liked and what they didn't so your next influencer campaign (no matter if it's with the same influencer or a different one) is more effective.

> **TIP**
>
> There are plenty of sentiment analysis tools available, and the Influencer Marketing Hub website is a good place to start your research:
>
> influencermarketinghub. com/best-sentiment-analysis-tools/

Monitor Brand Mentions and Social Media Impact

As part of tracking user sentiment, keep track of brand mentions, hashtags, and content created by your audience during the influencer campaign. Use that data to measure the reach and engagement of your campaign as well as the impact on your other online media, including your website and social media. Your influencer may have ideas for tracking audience activity as they probably have tools they already use.

Calculate the Financial ROI

All of the data we talk about collecting in this chapter needs to be applied to how many more sales the influencer marketing campaign generated. At a minimum, those calculations should include the sales revenue attributed to the campaign and the influencer's efforts, as well as the cost per acquisition (CPA) that's the result of the total investment divided by the amount of sales generated by the campaign. You may also want to track sales after the campaign for weeks or months afterward on different channels such as your website to see how long the campaign brings a return on your investment.

Not sure where to start? We recommend using the Rows website, which has dozens of built-in calculators including one for calculating influencer marketing ROI (see Figure 15-1). The calculator has some dummy numbers plugged into the form fields, and those can help you see the total revenue, cost, and ROI percentage. (rows.com/calculators/influencer-marketing-roi-calculator)

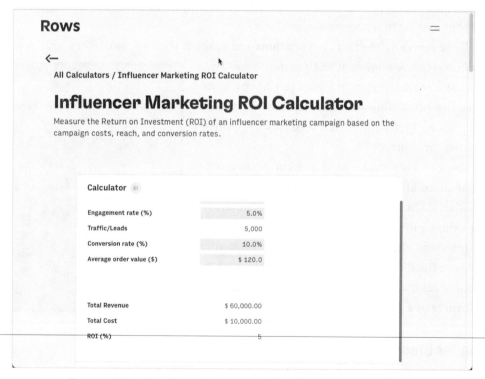

FIGURE 15-1. The Rows Influencer Marketing ROI Calculator.

Compare and Contrast

You can also establish benchmarks by comparing the performance of your influencer campaign to your previous marketing efforts as well as industry standards, if your industry has data on influencer marketing campaigns. For example, you can compare the engagement rates, website traffic, and conversions generated through the influencer campaign with your average and/or historical data.

What's more, you can create control groups that weren't exposed to the campaign to compare the control group's performance with the target audience for the influencer campaign. This can illuminate the effectiveness of the campaign and help isolate factors in the campaign that you may want to apply elsewhere in your marketing.

Remember that you won't get your influencer marketing ROI calculation right with the first influencer marketing campaign because there are a lot of quantitative and qualitative data that's specific to your business and industry. Your influencer, as well as your sales and marketing teams, will no doubt be able to help with that. But set expectations about the results early and often, especially if there are higher-ups who may have a "vending machine" mentality where they expect a certain result.

Going Micro for Macro Results

In Chapter 2, we introduced you to Tyler Anderson, the founder and CEO of the Casual Fridays marketing agency. He shared one example of setting measurable goals upfront when he worked with hospitality influencers. Tyler knew more than just tracking traditional metrics like followers or reach alone was needed—his clients needed to see sales translations.

One of Casual Fridays' resort clients is located right by Disneyland. With ambitions to boost bookings, they ran a campaign for that client leveraging top influencers in the Disney niche. Tyler didn't work with mega-influencers, but credible micro-influencers with dedicated Disney fan followings of 30,000 to 50,000 each. The resort hosted their stays, offering a behind-the-scenes sneak peek of the property alongside make-believe magic.

Naturally, Disney devotees took note. But more importantly, reservations started pouring in from the influencers' engaged audiences. Where typical efforts yielded awareness alone, now rooms were filling up. By tracking promotional codes used at checkout, Tyler's team proudly reported the solid bump in bookings attributable to these micro influencers. The client saw clear proof that influencer marketing was no necessary evil—the campaign delivered real ROI.

Small scale sweet success like this taught Tyler's agency the power of aligning niche passions, crafting win-win partnerships, and letting the results do the talking.

A Case Study: HotBox by Wiz

Ryan Baggott of the BaggottsBOTs Digital Marketing Agency in Bluffton, South Carolina (northeast of Savannah, Georgia), worked on an influencer campaign with rapper Wiz Khalifa in 2020. First, they created a ghost kitchen, which is a professional kitchen set up for delivery-only meals. Once the kitchen was ready, Ryan and Wiz launched HotBox by Wiz to provide various meals through food delivery services including DoorDash, Uber Eats, and Tap the Table.

Once the campaign was over, Ryan calculated the ROI and reported the following results.

- Over 100,000 Wiz Khalifa fans were captured in the automation we set up provided by the Tap the Table Facebook app.
- 9,900 fans proceeded to the next step in our marketing funnel, which was to subscribe to HotBox by Wiz.
- Of those 9,900 individuals, over 75 percent opted in for SMS, email marketing, or both.
- The Order Uber Eats button used in tracking conversions was clicked 770 times within a 39-day period.
- The average order value via UberEats held steady at $23 per order.
- 770 orders plus $23 on average per order equaled $20,900 in gross revenue from the campaign.

Ryan produced a presentation about the influencer campaign that you can find at express.adobe.com/page/xJe4VI6BWti6n/. The presentation also includes a YouTube commercial produced for HotBox by Wiz.

What You Learned

We've reached the end of the last chapter, and before you start planning your next (or first) influencer marketing campaign, let's review what you learned to make sure you have it all down.

As with any marketing endeavor, you need to set clear goals and preferences for your influencer marketing campaign before you start. Then you need to figure out what to measure, and those metrics can include reach, impressions, engagements, the conversion rate, and sales revenue.

Once you know what to track, you need to set up your trackers, such as unique promo codes for the campaign. You should consider using sentiment analysis tools to automatically gauge how well people are responding to your campaign. You also need to monitor what people are saying about your brand and the impact the campaign is having on social media.

After you gather your data, you can calculate the financial ROI of your campaign including sales revenue and the cost per acquisition. You should also consider tracking sales after the campaign officially ends to measure long-term effects, as well as compare your campaign performance with other marketing efforts.

Congratulations! You've come to the end of *Ultimate Guide to Influencer Marketing*, but this is just the beginning of your journey toward building profitable marketing campaigns that can grow your business faster than you ever thought possible. Go find your influencers!

About the Authors

ERIC BUTOW

Eric Butow is the owner of Butow Communications Group (BCG) in Jackson, California (https://www.butow.net). BCG was founded in 1994 and offers website development, online marketing, and writing services. He has authored or co-authored 45 books, most recently MCA Microsoft Office Specialist (Office 365 and Office 2019) Complete Study Guide (Sybex), Digital Etiquette for Dummies (Wiley), Instagram for Dummies, Second Edition (Wiley), Grow Your Business (Entrepreneur Press) and Write Your Business Plan, Second Edition (Entrepreneur Press). Eric has also developed and taught networking, computing, and usability courses for Ed2Go, Virtual Training Company, California State University, Sacramento, and Udemy.

When he's not working in (and on) his business or writing books, you can find Eric enjoying time with friends, walking around the historic Gold Rush town of Jackson, and helping his mother manage her infant and toddler daycare business.

STEPHANIE GARCIA

Stephanie Garcia is a live video strategist for brands and entrepreneurs–from moonwalkers to MasterChefs who want to go from unknown to unforgettable. A digital marketing expert with 15 years of ad agency experience, she has helped thousands of her clients and students get on the Fascination Fast Track™ to ignite their ideas and become confident on camera.

With her proven system, clients discover how to create crave-worthy content, get audiences buzzing with excitement, and deliver a spell-binding presentation that hooks viewers in.

Named one of the Top 50 Digital Marketing Thought Leaders by the University of Missouri St. Louis, her work has been recognized and awarded by Forbes, Online Marketing Media And Advertising, PR Daily, Forrester, and Gartner 1to1 Media.

She hosts Lights, Camera, and Live and co-authored Ultimate Guide to Social Media, published by Entrepreneur Press. She lives in San Diego, CA.

Influencer Marketing Resources

Here are many useful tools and resources referenced throughout the book and on the web that can help you with all aspects of your influencer marketing campaigns.

Articles and Insights

Britopian: britopian.com/
Keywordtool.io: keywordtool.io/
Influencer Marketing Hub: influencermarketinghub.com/
Neal Schaffer: nealschaffer.com/
U.S. Federal Trade Commission: www.ftc.gov/

Influencer Discovery
Capssion: capssion.com/
Heepsy: heepsy.com/
HypeAuditor: hypeauditor.com/
Julius: juliusworks.com/

Social Listening
Brandwatch: brandwatch.com/
Social Blade: socialblade.com/
SparkToro: sparktoro.com/

Outreach
Klear: klear.com/
NinjaOutreach: ninjaoutreach.com/
PitchBox: pitchbox.com/
Influencer Marketplaces

Collabster: collabstr.com/

Creator.co: creator.co/

CreatorIQ: creatoriq.com/

Influencer Stuff: influencerstuff.com/

Trend.io: trend.io/_____

Campaign Management

#paid: hashtagpaid.com/

Campaign Brief Template: canva.com/design/DAFvU-FWBak/bWyLY7K4zTNw-t1IIVzNfYg/view?utm_content=DAFvU-FWBak&utm_campaign=designshare&utm_medium=link&utm_source=publishsharelink

Influencer Marketing ROI Calculator: rows.com/calculators/influencer-marketing-roi-calculator

Influencity: influencity.com/

Klaia:joinklaia.com/

Later: later.com/

Mavrck: mavrck.co/

Referazon: referazon.com/

SARAL: getsaral.com/

Statusphere: joinstatus.com/

Traackr: traackr.com/

Upfluence: get.upfluence.com/

Influencer Tools for eCommerce Brands

Aspire: www.aspire.io/

GRIN: grin.co/

Influencer Marketing Agencies

62Above: 62above.com/

Audiencly: audiencly.com/

HireInfluence: hireinfluence.com/

Influencer Marketing Factory: theinfluencermarketingfactory.com/

Roberto Blake: robertoblake.com/

Glossary

above the line (ATL). Above the line marketing includes mass marketing strategies which are largely untargeted and are focused on building the brand.

accounts reached. Unique accounts who viewed the content.

activation. A marketing initiative to drive users to action through interactions and experiences.

actual impressions rate. The number of impressions divided by the number of total followers.

affiliate marketing. A marketing agreement between brand and influencer where the brand pays compensation to the influencer for generating traffic or leads through affiliate links to the brand website.

agency. Either a marketing agency that runs campaigns or a talent management agency that represents influencers.

algorithm. A detailed series of instructions for carrying out an operation on a computer. In terms of influencer marketing, companies use algorithms to determine or manipulate what content users of social media see in their feed and at what frequency.

always on. The campaign is occurring over a longer period of time as opposed to a single campaign or seasonal-specific timeline.

ambassador. An individual who represents a brand and can be the face of a campaign for a specified duration.

amplify. To drive additional distribution through optimized content.

audience. A group of people and social media users who follow and engage with an influencer.

audience insights. The different characteristics that define the audience of an influencer. These might be age, gender, location, occupation, etc.

benchmark. A point of reference to which things can be measured to determine success or failure.

brand advocate. A person who has a genuine affinity towards a brand and actively endorses or promotes the brand to their network both online and offline organically. Advocates are not always influencers.

brand awareness. The extent to which consumers are familiar with the distinctive qualities or image of a particular brand's goods and/or services.

Business to Business (B2B). A business that makes commercial transactions with another business.

Business to Consumer (B2C). A business who provides its services and products to the consumer market.

call to action (CTA). A message that aims to persuade the visitor (viewer, audience member, user) to pursue a certain action. Common examples of influencer CTAs are "like and comment" or "swipe up".

campaign. The tactical execution of a particular marketing strategy.

caption. The piece of text included in a post that describes it.

Click Through Rate (CTR). The ratio of users who click on a certain link to the number of total users who visit the page, post, or advertisement.

collaboration. The relationship between a brand and an influencer where the influencer produces content for the brand in exchange for compensation.

consideration. The extent to which consumers consider your brand for a given purchase occasion.

content calendar. A tool to plan content for publication in an influencer marketing campaign.

content marketing. The strategy of consistently producing high-quality content to engage a brand's audience.

conversion. The proportion of people viewing an advertisement and ending up making a purchase through the URL associated with the content. Conversion is measured by influencers using tracking links or promo codes.

cost equivalency metrics. The measurement of the value of influencer marketing investments as compared to other marketing disciplines.

Cost-Per-Acquisition (CPA). The metric that measures the cost of acquiring a customer or new user, which is calculated by dividing the total media investment by the number of acquisitions.

Cost-Per-Click (CPC). The metric that measures the cost of one customer clicking on an advertisement or link and landing on the company's website, which is calculated by dividing the campaign budget by the number of clicks.

Cost-Per-Engagement (CPE). The cost that is associated with each engagement or interaction, such as a like or comment. This is calculated by dividing the cost of the specific content by the total engagements it generates.

Cost-Per-Mille (CPM) or Cost-Per-Thousand (CPT). The cost per one thousand units, such as followers, video views, and/or impressions.

creator-centric. The process of building out your influencer marketing strategy with a deep understanding of the challenges faced by the talent you recruit for your campaign.

creative brief. A set of ideas that provides direction for content creation.

collaboration. A relationship between an influencer and a brand.

deliverables. The items that an influencer is expected to produce, as confirmed in the outreach and negotiation phase. The deliverables might be an Instagram post, a video showcasing your product, and/or coverage at an event, depending on the campaign.

disclosure. A visible indicator, such as a written text that is required to clearly state the purpose of the collaboration between the influencer and the brand. Common disclosures include words or hashtags such as ad, paid, in collaboration with, or sponsored.

distribution channel. The platform that is used to share content on.

earned media. The additional organic distribution generated from the media spend allocated to your influencer marketing campaign.

earned media value. The value of the additional organic distribution generated from your campaign with the assumption of a linear media distribution cost.

ecommerce. The commercial transactions that are conducted primarily on the Internet.

engagement. The practice of interacting with content.

engagement rate. A metric that determines the quality of an influencers content based on the number of interactions the content generates.

exclusivity. A specific right or restriction a brand or an agency might enact during the collaboration with an influencer.

flatlay. A style of photography often used by influencers when creating content about a brand they are collaborating with. Flatlays are styled images captured from above and usually portray a theme or group of items that can be used together.

feed. The platform interface where users view the content that is published by the people and influencers they follow.

follower range. The term to describe influencers based on how many followers they have. Influencer costs are usually based on their follower range.

full commercial content usage. The negotiated and secured terms to the right to use influencer generated content. That is, you have the right to use the content across your channels, but you do not own the content.

guest post. A website owner, such as a company, invites another writer to publish an article on their website. Brands often engage influencers to guest post on their website and/or blog as part of their influencer marketing strategy to create high-quality, engaging content on their platforms.

hashtag (#). A word or phrase preceded by a hash sign (#), which is used on social media and websites to identify content on a specific topic and are searchable keywords.

impressions. The number of views that a specific piece of content received over a specific period of time.

influencer. A creative person or group that has the ability to influence the behavior or opinions of others and may have an effect on a purchase decision in some significant or authoritative way.

influencer advertising. The discipline of leveraging influencer content by buying influencer content as media directly from influencers or through influencer marketplaces.

influencer compensation. The method by which an influencer is paid for their time, expertise, or partnership with a brand. Although some compensation is monetary, compensation can also include offering the influencer experiences, trips, or free product.

influencer endorsement. The approval for a brand's product or service, integrated into the influencer's content in a way that generates awareness for the brand.

Influencer-Generated Content (IGC). A piece of content an influencer creates that mentions a brand. Similar to user-generated content (UGC), IGC is authentic content created by a person mentioning the brand's products or services.

influencer marketing. The practice of connecting influential individuals with the right target audience and with relevant brands to help the brand communicate their message to achieve its marketing objective.

influencer marketing platform. A tool that helps influencers and brands manage the influencer marketing process.

influencer marketplace. A technology that aims to match brands and participating influencers based on simple criteria, facilitate fulfillment of paid activities through standardized processes, and provide KPIs that attempt to mimic campaign performance measures.

influencer profile. A model example of key characteristics a type of influencer would possess. These characteristics may include the size of following, current relationship status with the brand, the type of content they create, and how they like to be engaged.

influencer rate card. An outline of an influencer's service costs, which generally reflects the cost of content integrations and sponsored posts.

Influencer Relationship Management (IRM). The process of building and managing long-term relationships with a select group of influencers, which is often described as customer resource management (CRM) for marketers. IRM programs work to increase the positive mentions of your brand among select opinion leaders for higher brand visibility.

influencer representation. Agents who represent influencers and manage an influencer's collaborations, deals, and contracts with brands and agencies.

influencer vetting. The process of evaluating influencers based on performance, audience quality, and value alignment.

Instagram Stories. An Instagram feature that allows users to upload a picture or a video on their profile. The story expires after twenty-four hours unless it's highlighted on the account profile page.

Instagram takeover. An influencer takes responsibility for a brand's Instagram account for a short period of time to share content with the brand's audience from their perspective.

integrated. When a piece of content references multiple brands.

Key Performance Indicator (KPI). The trackable and quantifiable metric that is used to evaluate the goals of an influencer marketing campaign.

licensing. Acquiring the right to use influencer content based on permissions or usage rights.

link in bio. A phrase and call to action (CTA) that an influencer uses to signal to their audience that they have put more information in their bio.

macro-influencer. An influencer with a larger following on one or several of their active platforms.

Mommy Blogger. A woman who shares her parenting, family, and motherhood journey with her community via a blog and/or social platforms. Mommy bloggers are considered a core target market by many brands for influencer marketing campaigns.

Multi-Channel Network (MCN). A company or entity that works with multiple channels and content creators.

media kit. A digital document that acts as a CV or résumé for influencers. A media kit contains information about the influencer, previous experience, skills, channels, and followers.

media spend. The budget invested in an influencer marketing campaign.

micro-influencer. An influencer with a smaller but usually a highly engaged audience (typically 10K-100K followers).

Most Valuable Distribution (MVD). A brand's most effective channel strategy and the best practice unique for their brand, which yields the greatest return on investment with the lowest amount of effort.

monetize. The process of converting services or assets into a stream of revenue.

multi-tiered approach. The approach that strategically leverages various influencers across different audience sizes to ensure all key performance indicators are met.

niche. A small segment in the market of population with unique and/or very specific characteristics or needs.

off brand. When content does not align to the value a brand is aiming to achieve.

organic. In an influencer marketing campaign, this refers to something that happened naturally without intervention via a paid model.

organic content. This content is not sponsored by the brand and holds no material connection to it.

optimize. To make the influencer marketing content perform better to meet the campaign KPI.

outreach. The process of connecting with influencers about potential collaborations.

owned media. Branded content published on the brand's own channels.

page views. The metric used to show how many views a page on a website received during a specified period of time.

paid content. Also known as sponsored content, the cost for producing the content that is covered in whole or in part by a sponsoring brand advertiser.

paid media. Any media coverage or advertising that you have paid for as part of your marketing strategy.

paid post. A blog or social media post that has been paid to be produced. Often paid posts are produced by influencers in collaboration with a brand in exchange for a form of compensation.

paid reach. The number of impressions of content, such as a YouTube video, that have been earned through a paid content model.

personal brand. The personal features, values, and qualities of an influencer. When influencers consider working with a brand, they ensure that the brand aligns with their own personal brand to ensure authentic content for their audiences.

participation rate. The numbers of influencers who join one or more of your influencer marketing campaigns.

plandid. A photo that appears candid and casual but is actually strategically planned and shot to look that way.

platform. A social media channel or website where users post content.

podcast. Audio content that is delivered in a regular series, usually around a particular topic or theme and/or featuring the same talent.

poll interaction rate. The share of an audience interacting with the Vote feature in Instagram Stories.

product integration. The integration of a brand's specific product through explicitly introducing, including, and mentioning it within the influencer's content.

public relations. An industry within the marketing and advertising space that specializes in securing media coverage for their clients including brands, businesses, and personalities.

qualification. The process of evaluating influencers for their suitability for a specific brand influence marketing campaign.

reach. The total number of followers an influencer or a brand has. This may be on a specific social platform or combined on all their platforms.

relevance. A measure of how relevant an influencer is to a topic that is relevant to your brand.

Return on Investment (ROI). The total value received on a marketing investment. In influencer marketing, the ROI shows the success of the campaign and the measure of success depends on the campaign goal.

Search Engine Optimization (SEO). The practice of increasing your website's visibility in search results on search engines.

segment. A specific group of influencers differentiated by the type of content they create, or by the specific audience demographics they reach, such as lifestyle, fashion, parenting, and travel.

sentiment. An opinion, either positive, negative, or neutral that is openly expressed. In an influencer marketing campaign, sentiment is used to analyze the audience's response to a brand or influencer content.

sentiment analysis. The process to identify opinions expressed by followers within the comments in response to influencer content, which helps to determine attitudes towards a particular topic or product.

share-of-voice. The percentage or portion of the conversation with target consumers or influencers your brand owns versus your competitors. This conversation can be on social media platforms, blogs, or any other place your target audience hears from brands.

social commerce. A rising subset of ecommerce that is enabled by social media, and often facilitated by influencers. Social commerce tools include augmented reality, live shopping abilities, direct social shopping experiences, and influencer marketplaces.

social media. A collective term that describes websites and apps that allow users to create content and share it with their audience.

social media platform. An online platform that allows users to socialize and connect with one another. Examples include Facebook, Instagram, LinkedIn, and X (formerly Twitter).

swipe up. The feature on both Instagram Stories that allows the user to link to a website from their post so that their audience can get more specific information.

tag. A link within a post that links to another user's page on the platform. A tag is usually a username preceded by the @ symbol.

target audience. The ideal group of consumers that a brand wants to attract with an influencer marketing campaign.

Terms of Service (TOS). The terms or rules that have to be agreed upon between a brand and its customers before using a product or a service.

total accounts reached. Total unique accounts that viewed a piece of content.

total content engagement. The sum of all shares, likes, and comments about a piece of content.

total digital audience. The total sum of an influencer's potential reach across all their active social platforms as well as all monthly unique visits to their blog, if applicable.

tracking links. URLs that are used to direct traffic to a landing page from somewhere other than a website. Tracking links are included in influencer marketing campaigns to help brands track, measure, and report the success of a campaign.

User-Generated Content (UGC). Any form of content created and shared organically by customers or users.

unique visitor. The term used to measure the number of distinct individuals requesting pages from a website during a given period of time.

views. The number of users who have watched a piece of content.

webinar. A webinar is a seminar conducted over the internet where participants tune in via a unique link or login to access the content.

YouTuber. A digital influencer with a large and active presence on YouTube and an engaged community of subscribers.

Index

D

metrics, 91–92, 119–120

    See also key performance indicators (KPIs)

micro-influencers

    described, 42, 138

    Instagram and, 16–17

    number of followers, 41

    rates and, 8, 41

    reaching out to, 45–52

mid-tier influencers, 41–42

mommy bloggers, xi, 138

monetization, 19, 138

N

nano-influencers, 8, 41–44, 45, 46

negative publicity, 97

niche markets, 16–17, 138

Notion, 58

Nyst, Annabelle, 4–5

O

Omnisend, 58

one percent rule, 78

opportunities, 75, 76

opt-in mechanisms, 115

Opus Clip, 111

outposts, 79

outreach messages

    Capssion, 54–55

    direct messages (DMs), 47, 48–49, 50